YP 303.48 MOR
Morin, I_____ ___ 1928-
Women wh____
D0442241

In Memory

Of

Our Son

Timothy Ahearn

MONTROSE LIBRARY DISTRICT

1 11 0001367821

Women Who Reformed Politics

Women Who Reformed Politics

Isobel V. Morin

The Oliver Press, Inc.
Minneapolis

MONTROSE LIBRARY DISTRICT
434 South First Street
Montrose, Colorado 81401

Copyright © 1994 by The Oliver Press, Inc.

All rights reserved. No part of this book may be reproduced in any form or by any means without permission in writing from the publisher. Please address inquiries to:

The Oliver Press, Inc.
Josiah King House
2709 Lyndale Avenue South
Minneapolis, MN 55408

Library of Congress Cataloging-in-Publication Data

Morin, Isobel V., 1928-

Women who reformed politics / Isobel V. Morin.
p. cm. — (Profiles)
Includes bibliographical references and index.
ISBN 1-881508-16-1 : $14.95
1. Women social reformers—United States—Biography—Juvenile
literature. [1. Reformers. 2. Women—Biography.] I. Title.
II. Series: Profiles (Minneapolis, Minn.)
HQ1412.M67 1994
303.48'4'0922—dc20
[B]   93-46336
                                                                 CIP
                                                                  AC

ISBN: 1-881508-16-1
Profiles XI
Printed in the United States of America

99 98 97 96 95 94   8 7 6 5 4 3 2 1

Contents

Introduction 7

Chapter 1   Abby Kelley Foster:
             A Crusader against Slavery 13

Chapter 2   Frances Willard:
             A Voice for Temperance 29

Chapter 3   Ida Wells-Barnett:
             A Fighter against Mob Violence............45

Chapter 4   Carrie Chapman Catt:
             Getting the Right to Vote......................61

Chapter 5   Molly Dewson:
             A Political Boss 79

Chapter 6   Pauli Murray:
             Ahead of the Crowd...............................97

Chapter 7   Fannie Lou Hamer:
             Civil Rights Champion 113

Chapter 8   Gloria Steinem:
             A Liberated Woman 129

Major Reforms in U.S. History 145

Bibliography..149

Index...153

Gloria Steinem (with megaphone), one of the most recent in a long line of women to fight for social change, speaks out at a 1979 rally for women's rights.

Introduction

*T*hroughout much of American history, women couldn't take part in the formal political process. Before the adoption of the Nineteenth Amendment in 1920, only 15 states allowed women to vote or hold public office, and many schools and professions didn't admit women. Most women accepted this state of affairs. Believing that their primary responsibility was the care of their families and homes, they left the world of business and politics to men. Occasionally, however, a few bold women became convinced that some aspect of society needed reform and ventured into the male-dominated world of public affairs.

During the 1830s and 1840s, many women joined the growing movement to abolish slavery. Most limited themselves to activities that society considered appropriate for women, such as attending meetings of women's groups, organizing fund-raising events, and encouraging male friends and relatives in their abolitionist activities. A small number of women, however, violated the social norms of the day by publicly campaigning for an end to slavery.

By the 1850s, women began to push for improvements in state laws concerning marriage, divorce, child custody, and the right of married women to own property and control their finances. They fought for increased access to education, more career opportunities and, above all, the right to vote.

As the nineteenth century drew to a close, increasing numbers of women viewed their traditional role as caretakers of their families and homes in a broader light. They came to believe that their responsibility also included the elimination of social ills that adversely influenced the home and family. These reforming women tried to correct a variety of social problems that affected the community's moral, economic, and social welfare. Women campaigned for reforms such as restrictions on the sale of alcoholic beverages, better working conditions for women, restrictions on child labor, and improved public education, sanitation, and recreational facilities.

The Nineteenth Amendment offered new challenges for women because voting rights didn't automatically give them a representative share of political power. They still had barriers to break. Some women attacked these roadblocks by campaigning for (and sometimes winning) elective public office. Others worked from the sidelines to gain full participation in the country's economic and political life. Some women reformers worked to end formal discrimination in areas such as voting rights, education, and employment. Others tried to change public attitudes that fostered discrimination.

Whatever reforms these women embraced, sooner or later most of them saw a connection between other social problems and the second-class status held by women. This was especially true for those who worked to ensure racial justice. These reformers often saw racial and gender discrimination as opposite sides of the same coin. Believing that only a two-pronged attack would bring progress in combating racial and gender biases, they decided to fight against both forms of discrimination.

This book looks at eight women who were active in reforming the political system of the United States. Although none of these women ever held public office, they nonetheless influenced political change.

Some of these women preferred to meet a problem head on rather that compromise on an issue. But often these boat-rockers were unsuccessful. Other women adopted a more moderate approach. Believing that half a loaf was better than none, they were willing to accept compromises in order to achieve their goals. The compromisers often succeeded over time. However, their successes often resulted from the efforts of their more confrontational colleagues.

Some of the reforms that these women struggled for were considered controversial because many people at the time did not agree with them. Because of this, some of the reformers reached their goals only after prolonged struggle. Other reformers, regardless of the methods they used, failed during the short term but succeeded in the long run because they paved the way for later groups to achieve the desired reform.

Today, many women (and also men) continue to fight for reforms. Some people join organizations that support a particular public interest. They may write letters to newspapers or legislative representatives to persuade elected officials to vote a certain way. They may also donate or solicit money for election campaigns and canvass voters by making telephone calls or going door-to-door. These informal, grassroots activities involving ordinary citizens sometimes exert a greater influence on public policy than actions taken by political parties and politicians.

Today's reformers still haven't achieved all of their goals. Issues such as improving access to child care for working women, receiving equal pay for equal work, allowing women the right to control their reproductive function, and combating sexual harassment in the workplace remain difficult and divisive issues among U.S. citizens. Regardless of the degree of their success, however, today's reformers are living evidence of the enduring struggle to improve the lives of all Americans.

Although most women worked only in the home during the nineteenth century, Abby Kelley Foster (1811-1887) traveled across the United States to speak out against slavery.

1

Abby Kelley Foster
A Crusader against Slavery

*A*t a time when most women stayed home and took care of their families and households, Abby Kelley was considered a troublemaker. This New England Quaker roamed the countryside speaking out against slavery. Abby Kelley Foster seemed to delight in making the most outrageous accusations against the government, the clergy, and anyone else who failed to demand an immediate end to what the South called its "peculiar institution." Even other abolitionists sometimes regarded her as a crackpot.

Abigail Kelley hadn't always been so outspoken. Born on January 15, 1811, near Pelham, Massachusetts, she was almost 27 when she first felt compelled to crusade against slavery. In the spring of 1811, her family moved to Worcester, 40 miles east of Pelham, where Abby grew up. Since she had six older sisters (and no older brothers), young Abby wasn't tied to the usual round of household jobs that most girls faced. Instead, she had time to help her father with the outdoor chores around the small family farm. After her brother, Albert, was born in 1813 and her older sisters began to marry and leave home, her responsibilities at home increased. Still, the comparative freedom Abby Kelley enjoyed during early childhood helped to develop the independent spirit that was so evident in her later years.

Abby's Quaker upbringing also aided her independence. The members of the Society of Friends (commonly called Quakers) didn't believe in hiring clergy or holding formal religious services. Instead, they attended religious meetings where both men and women spoke as their own "inner light" prompted them to address the group. Quakers believe all people have an inner light that guides them to do what is right. Abby's Quaker religion freed her from the restrictions that many other churches imposed on their female members in the early nineteenth century.

Abby Kelley also had a better education than many girls at that time. In 1826, after attending a one-room school, she left Massachusetts for a Quaker boarding school in Providence, Rhode Island. There she studied algebra, botany, astronomy, and bookkeeping, in addition to the traditional "Three R's"—reading, 'riting, and 'rithmetic. Toward the end of 1829, Abby returned home to teach school. Her earnings helped to support her aging parents and paid the tuition for her brother, Albert, and younger sister Lucy to attend the Providence school.

In 1832, an event occurred that changed Abby Kelley's life. That year, a man named William Lloyd Garrison came to Worcester to give an antislavery lecture. Garrison, the editor of the *Liberator*, a new weekly newspaper, said slavery was a sin and demanded that it be immediately abolished. The fiery young orator also believed that black Americans should have the same civil and political rights as whites.

Garrison's speech impressed Kelley, but she wasn't ready yet to support his antislavery crusade; his ideas were well outside the American mainstream. At that time, most white Americans accepted slavery as a normal aspect of human existence. Even many people who opposed slavery thought it should end gradually, and they hoped the freed slaves could be encouraged to migrate to Liberia, a U.S.-sponsored colony in West Africa.

In 1836, Kelley moved to Lynn, Massachusetts, not far from Boston, for a new teaching job. By that time, Garrison's American Anti-Slavery Society, founded in 1833, had attracted a large following. Shortly after her

Newspaper editor William Lloyd Garrison (1805-1879) persuaded many people to join the abolition movement.

arrival in Lynn, Abby Kelley joined the Lynn Female Anti-Slavery Society and soon became its corresponding secretary. That office kept her in touch with other antislavery organizations.

In the summer of 1836, Kelley and a friend she was boarding with did a very daring thing. They went door to door asking people to sign a petition demanding that Congress put an end to slavery in the District of Columbia. Many people thought door-to-door canvassing was inappropriate for women. Still, the two women persisted. In Kelley's opinion, distributing petitions was an effective way of spreading the antislavery message—regardless of how many people signed them.

Abby Kelley's life changed dramatically after her father died in December 1836. His death left Kelley deeply shaken, and she began to question the purpose of her existence. A long time passed before she found an answer to that question. Eventually, she decided that God was calling her to speak out against the evils that afflicted humanity, especially the evil of slavery.

Kelley's first venture into public speaking before an audience of both men and women was literally a baptism of fire. In May 1838, she went to Philadelphia for a convention of antislavery women. The convention turned into a disaster. During an evening session, a mob of men and boys surrounded the meeting place, screaming, cursing, and pelting the windows with rocks.

The first shipload of black Africans reached North America in 1619, and white Southerners continued to keep blacks as slaves into the nineteenth century.

The situation was chaotic as Kelley rose and addressed the large group. The crash of broken glass punctuated her words as she urged her audience to work on behalf of the slaves. Although she had previously spoken publicly only in front of small groups of women and hadn't been scheduled to speak that night, her speech impressed those inside the building. The mob outside, however, continued to shout threats, so the mayor of Philadelphia ordered the women to leave the building. The last of them were scarcely out the door before the mob burned the meeting hall to the ground.

Although the episode reinforced Kelley's belief that God was calling her to speak out against slavery, she wasn't ready to begin traveling yet. Her mother was ill, and Kelley went home to care for her. In 1838, however, Kelley left her sister Lucy in charge of their ailing mother and moved to Connecticut to spread the anti-slavery message. Using her sister Olive's home as a base of operations, she traveled around the state by stage-coach or on foot, speaking wherever she could find a lecture room and staying overnight with anyone willing to take her in.

By that time, the abolition movement was coming apart at the seams because of differences of opinion among its members. One bone of contention was the role of women in the movement. Another was whether the abolitionists should take political action to force an end to slavery or follow William Lloyd Garrison's example of using persuasion. Garrison's opposition to political action, his attacks on the federal government and the Constitution (which he saw as corrupt supporters of slavery), and his support of women's active membership in the antislavery societies had angered some abolitionists. Instead of cooperating to promote their common cause, the abolitionists began hurling insults at one another.

Things came to a head in May 1840, when a group of abolitionists who disagreed with Garrison dropped out of the American Anti-Slavery Society and formed a new organization, the American and Foreign Anti-Slavery Society. Women could join the new group, but they couldn't vote or hold office. Also, the group refused to admit as members people who disagreed strongly with the U.S. government.

Many of Garrison's opponents blamed Kelley for the split between the rival abolitionist groups. A talented speaker, organizer, and fund raiser, she had taken an increasingly active part in Garrison's organization. His opponents, in fact, used the phrase "Abby Kelleyism" to describe the actions of women who refused to "stay in their place." When Abby Kelley persisted in stumping for an end to slavery, her opponents accused her of serving Satan. Her public speaking before mixed audiences—which some members of the clergy condemned as an unnatural attempt to assume a man's place—was bad enough. But her practice of traveling without a chaperone was completely outrageous. Abby Kelley had become notorious.

During this period, the Society of Friends seemed to turn against the abolitionists. Many Quakers barred antislavery speakers from their meeting houses and discouraged their members from joining antislavery societies. Because of this, Kelley resigned from the Quakers early in 1841. A few months later, the group disowned her.

That summer, Kelley went to Concord, New Hampshire, to attend the annual meeting of that state's antislavery society. One of the speakers was a former theological student named Stephen Symonds Foster. The young orator, who was born in New Hampshire in 1809, had been lecturing for the New Hampshire society for

Because she was a woman, Abby Kelley Foster was not accepted by many men in the abolition movement.

two years. The two people were immediately attracted to each other; they were kindred spirits, uncompromising in their zeal for the cause and skilled in the art of hurling insults at their opponents.

Because both were unwilling to let their personal feelings interfere with the task at hand, a long time passed before the pair admitted their love for each other and still longer before they set a wedding date. In December 1845, Abby Kelley and Stephen Foster took a brief vacation from their antislavery work in Ohio and crossed the state line into Pennsylvania, where they got married on December 21.

21

Stephen Foster (1809-1881) and his wife, Abby, were often willing to put their abolition work ahead of their personal lives.

By late 1846, Abby Kelley Foster was pregnant. Clearly, she would have to take a break from the endless round of road trips that had kept them busy since their wedding. In April 1847, Stephen Foster bought a house in Worcester, and the couple's only child, Paulina Wright Foster, was born in their new home one month later.

The birth, however, caused only a temporary interruption in the Fosters' travels. At least one of Paulina's parents was on the road much of the time campaigning for an end to slavery, but the Fosters had plenty of relatives available for baby-sitting.

By mid-century, the Fosters were fighting for a second cause. A meeting of a small group of women in Seneca Falls, New York, in 1848 to discuss women's rights had generated a full-scale women's rights movement. In 1850 and 1851, the women's rights group held conventions in Worcester. Abby Kelley Foster took an active part in both meetings. Afterward, she continued to support the push for women's rights but concerned herself primarily with the abolition of slavery.

During the 1850s, many of Garrison's supporters softened their stand against politics and supported the Republican party, which began as a coalition of different groups that opposed any further spread of slavery into the American territories. The Fosters didn't agree with their fellow abolitionists' support for a political party, and they continued to speak out against the government and slavery until well after the beginning of the Civil War. In 1864, Abby Kelley Foster objected to the Anti-Slavery Society's support of President Abraham Lincoln's reelection on the grounds that such support would turn the antislavery organization into a political party.

In all her years as an abolitionist, Abby Kelley Foster abandoned her antipolitical stance only once. After the

Secretary of State William Seward watches as President Abraham Lincoln signs the 1863 Emancipation Proclamation, one of the federal government's first steps to end slavery.

passage of the Thirteenth Amendment in 1865, which outlawed slavery, many abolitionists considered their job done. Foster disagreed, believing that the freed slaves needed the right to vote to protect their newly won freedom. Once again, she backed an unpopular cause. Because many northerners thought that blacks were not capable of voting in a responsible manner, few states in the North allowed blacks to vote on an equal basis with whites.

Foster's support of voting rights for black men also alienated some women's rights advocates who wanted women to have the right to vote. Women's suffragists such as Susan B. Anthony and Elizabeth Cady Stanton argued, sometimes with racist overtones, that the government shouldn't give black men voting rights ahead of white women. But Foster insisted that giving black men the right to vote should come first. In her opinion, they had suffered greater wrongs than white women and therefore had a greater claim to remedial action. She believed, moreover, that the former slaves would never be completely free until they had the right to vote.

In spite of the opposition of some suffragists, Foster campaigned in support of the Fifteenth Amendment, which forbade the federal and state governments from denying or abridging men's right to vote because of their race, color, or previous condition of servitude. In February 1870, her efforts were rewarded when Texas

Elizabeth Cady Stanton (1815-1902) and other women's rights advocates of the nineteenth century argued that white women should receive the right to vote before black men.

became the 28th state to vote in favor of the amendment, making it part of the Constitution.

The disbanding of the American Anti-Slavery Society after the Fifteenth Amendment's ratification left the Fosters free to retire to private life. However, the pair had one more spark of protest left in their aging bodies. In 1873, they decided not to pay taxes on their farm and personal property until Massachusetts gave Abby Kelley Foster the right to vote. They carried on a running battle with the Worcester tax collector until 1880, when they gave up and paid their taxes. By that time, Stephen Foster had become too ill to continue the fight.

Stephen Foster died on September 8, 1881. His widow lived for another five years. After spending the last months of her life writing a biographical sketch of her late husband, Abby Kelley Foster died on January 14, 1887, one day short of her 76th birthday.

Foster, who so often expressed her distaste for politics and politicians, was a thoroughly political woman. Her political skills as an organizer, fund raiser, and debater made her an effective lobbyist for both the abolition of slavery and voting rights for black men. This reformer influenced the world of politics during the nineteenth century without ever voting or holding public office.

Convinced that alcohol abuse contributed to many social problems, Frances Willard (1839-1898) became one of the strongest leaders of the temperance movement during the nineteenth century.

2

Frances Willard
A Voice for Temperance

*I*n the summer of 1859, a young Midwestern woman confided to her diary, "Have I told you I was going away to earn my own living, fight my own battles, and be a felt force in the world?" Those were ambitious words. At that time, few unmarried middle-class women held paying jobs, and an even a smaller number lived independently. Frances Elizabeth Willard, who was approaching her 20th birthday, was about to take the bold step of leaving her parents' comfortable house on the shores of Lake Michigan to teach in a one-room schoolhouse about 15 miles away, even though her father, a prosperous banker, was well able to support her.

Frances Willard, the second of Josiah and Mary Hill Willard's three children, was born in the town of Churchville, New York, on September 28, 1839. When she was two years old, her family moved to Oberlin, Ohio, where Josiah studied for the ministry at Oberlin College. When Josiah Willard became ill in 1846, his doctor advised him to give up his theological studies and move to the open countryside. Because of this, the family then moved to a 360-acre farm in Janesville, in the territory of Wisconsin, a few miles north of the Illinois line.

Young Frances (or "Frank," as she liked to be called) was relatively free during her years on the farm. Although her mother insisted on strict obedience to household rules, she gave daughters Frank and Mary considerable leeway in choosing their activities. Frank, who preferred outdoor activities to household chores, didn't learn such "womanly" arts as cooking and sewing until she was in her teens. By that time, she had also learned to ride a horse and was skilled in carpentry.

During the family's first few years in Wisconsin, Mary Willard, who had worked as a schoolteacher for 11 years before her marriage, taught her daughters at home, while Frank's older brother, Oliver, attended school in Janesville. Mary Willard encouraged her two young pupils to keep journals to improve their writing. Frank spent many hours reading from the family's small library and writing in her diary—activities that helped to develop the writing skills that would become important to her during her later life.

In the spring of 1857, when Frank was 17, she and 14-year-old Mary left home to attend a boarding school in Milwaukee, where their mother's sister worked as a teacher. They stayed for only one school term because Josiah Willard, who had never liked the idea of sending his daughters away to school, refused to allow them to return. At the end of the year, however, he agreed to send the young women to the North Western Female College, a Methodist-affiliated school in Evanston, Illinois, near the recently opened Northwestern University. In the summer of 1858, the family moved to Evanston, and Frank and Mary completed their education as day students.

While attending North Western Female College, Frank Willard was a rebellious student. Never one to accept anything on faith, she began to question the religious doctrines she had learned as a child. In January 1860, however, she put aside her religious doubts and formally joined the Methodist church. She remained a member of the church the rest of her life.

Young Frances Willard also questioned the roles society assigned to men and women. At that time, people believed that a woman's responsibilities were limited to the care of her children and home, whereas a man's responsibilities included civic and political affairs, as well as the financial support of his family. Willard eventually adopted the view that, in addition to caring for the home, women also needed to reform any social conditions that threatened their homes and families.

After her graduation in 1859, Willard taught school in Harlem and Kankakee, Illinois. In the spring of 1861, she became engaged to Charles Fowler, one of her brother's classmates at Garrett Theological Seminary in Evanston. Young Fowler, who would later become a university president, newspaper editor, and Methodist bishop, was handsome and intelligent. He also strongly believed in male dominance, an attitude that proved too much for his fiancée. In 1862 Frank Willard broke the engagement.

For the next few years, Willard moved from one teaching job to another, never staying long in one place. Meanwhile, her father's health was deteriorating. In 1867, he returned to his boyhood home in Churchville, where he died in January 1868. Although Frances Willard grieved over her father's death, she did not stop from moving on with her life.

In the spring of 1868, Willard and her close friend and fellow teacher, Kate Jackson, sailed for Europe. The two women were away from the United States for more than two years, spending their time sightseeing and study- ing. They toured the British Isles, Europe, North Africa, and the Middle East. When they returned home in September 1870, Willard, who had learned French,

A firm believer in education, Frances Willard had an impressive career as a teacher.

Frances Willard (center) poses here with her mother and sister—both of whom were named Mary.

German, and Italian during her travels, was ready to advance her teaching career.

Her opportunity came in 1870, when she became president of Evanston Ladies College. The college, organized in 1869 as a successor to North Western Female College, was affiliated with Northwestern University. In 1873, the two institutions merged. Willard became a professor at Northwestern and dean of its new Woman's College.

Around that time, Northwestern's president resigned to accept another job. His replacement was Charles Fowler, Frances Willard's former fiancé. Fowler narrowed her authority in the Woman's College and Northwestern's male students, unused to the idea of a female professor, engaged in a campaign of petty harassment against her. Willard realized she could not stay there, and she resigned from the college in 1874.

Now almost 35 years old, Willard had to find a new means of support for herself and her mother. Her sister, Mary, had died in 1862, and her brother was unable to help because he had financial problems of his own as well as a severe drinking problem.

Oliver Willard's struggle with alcohol may have influenced Frances Willard's choice of a new occupation, one she would have for the rest of her life. Shortly after leaving Northwestern, she became active in the newly formed Woman's Christian Temperance Union, an organization that wanted to reduce the consumption of alcohol.

For many years, the temperance movement had played a prominent role in American politics. Prior to the Civil War, temperance advocates had succeeded in getting many state and local governments to pass temperance laws restricting or prohibiting the sale of alcoholic beverages. Most of these temperance laws were later repealed, however. In the period following the end of the Civil War, few laws regulated the alcoholic beverage industry.

Americans reacted to the problem of excessive drinking in a variety of ways. Some clergymen asked their congregations to abstain from the use of alcohol and urge others to follow their example. Likewise, many people sought a legal solution to the problem of excessive drinking. In 1869, a group of temperance advocates formed the Prohibition party, which endorsed a complete ban on the liquor trade. In 1874, some American women decided to attack the problem in their own way by starting a temperance crusade.

The new temperance crusade began in western New York state and in the Midwest as a series of demonstrations; groups of women, praying and singing hymns, marched to the saloons to beg both owners and customers to mend their ways. Many of the women knelt to pray in the streets or inside the saloons. Some of the women placed their open bibles on the bars.

In 1874, the demonstrators held a convention in Cleveland, Ohio, where they formed the national Woman's Christian Temperance Union (WCTU). The new organization became the training ground for countless reforming women in the late nineteenth century, and Frances Willard became its most influential leader. In September that year, Willard became president of the Chicago WCTU. The following month, she became secretary of the Illinois WCTU, and in November she became corresponding secretary of the newly formed National WCTU.

Willard's experience with the WCTU transformed her life. She left behind the orderly existence of an educator for the hectic life of an organizer, writer, lecturer, and political activist. She traveled extensively throughout the United States, speaking about temperance and helping to organize new WCTU chapters. She wrote numerous articles for WCTU publications as well as several books, including her autobiography and a biography of her mother, who died in 1892.

Willard's political thinking gradually evolved during the 1870s and 1880s. Already a believer in women's suffrage, she became convinced that giving women the right to vote—at least on questions involving the manufacture and sale of alcoholic beverages—would also benefit the temperance cause. She called this voting right the "Home Protection Ballot," arguing that women needed it to protect their homes from the dangers of alcohol. She also became convinced that a constitutional amendment prohibiting the manufacture and sale of alcoholic beverages was the only way to ensure temperance.

Meanwhile, Willard was expanding her influence in the WCTU. In 1879, she became president of its national organization, an office she would hold for the rest of her life. She also enlarged the WCTU's membership in both numbers and in geographical scope. Through her efforts, the WCTU's membership spread into the South and West. She also helped to form an international women's temperance organization, called World's WCTU, and in 1891 she became its first president.

During the 1880s and 1890s, Willard became increasingly active in politics. She served on the Prohibition party's executive committee from 1882 to 1891. In 1882, she persuaded the party to endorse voting rights for women, and in 1885, she persuaded the WCTU to endorse the Prohibition party. Although women couldn't vote, Willard hoped the WCTU's endorsement would influence men to support the Prohibitionists. In 1892, Willard tried unsuccessfully to get the new People's party (commonly called the Populist party) to endorse both women's suffrage and prohibition.

During her tenure as president of the American WCTU, Willard adopted the slogan "Do Everything." She originally meant that the WCTU should use every means at its disposal to achieve its goal of temperance. Gradually, however, she shifted the slogan's emphasis to one of endorsing multiple reforms. Under her leadership, the WCTU fought for such causes as women's suffrage,

As an adult, Frances Willard became an avid bicycle rider—which she considered a sign of personal independence.

labor and prison reform, public health and hygiene, and new laws regarding prostitution and rape.

Both her do-everything policy and her political activities were controversial, however. To complicate matters, when Willard lived abroad for long periods during the 1890s, many women thought she was neglecting her duties as president of the American WCTU. By the middle of the decade, she faced a growing rebellion in the WCTU ranks. Despite this, Willard remained popular with most WCTU members, who convinced their leaders to keep her on as president.

Willard, however, was suffering from pernicious anemia and her health was deteriorating. After presiding over the WCTU's national convention in 1897, she moved into a New York hotel with her secretary and longtime friend, Anna Gordon. Willard soon became bedridden and died on February 17, 1898. After her death, flags flew at half-mast in both Chicago and Washington in tribute to this reforming woman. In 1905, the people of Illinois placed her statue in the U.S. Capitol's Statuary Hall.

Willard's policies didn't survive her, however. After her death, the WCTU abandoned her do-everything policy and concentrated on promoting its traditional goals: encouraging people to stop drinking alcoholic beverages and lobbying the government to prohibit the manufacture and sale of alcohol.

Anna Gordon, Frances Willard's secretary and close friend, helped care for the temperance leader during her final days.

This strategy was successful. In 1919, through the combined efforts of the WCTU, the Prohibition party, and the Anti-Saloon League (formed in 1893), Congress passed the Eighteenth Amendment, which prohibited the manufacture, sale, or transportation of intoxicating liquors in the United States and its territories. The amendment took effect in January 1920 after its ratification by 36 of the 48 states.

The experiment with Prohibition proved to be an unfortunate one, however. A thriving underworld soon arose out of the illegal liquor business. Gang wars, which many people blamed on the bootleg liquor trade, erupted on city streets. The unregulated liquor industry often sold contaminated products that blinded or killed their users. In 1933, Prohibition (which Americans had never completely supported) ended with the passage of the Twenty-first Amendment.

Although alcohol consumption declined during the time of Prohibition, most people now regard Prohibition as a failed policy because of the crime that accompanied it. There is a growing awareness, however, that the problem of alcohol abuse that Frances Willard and her colleagues tried to correct during the nineteenth century is all too real today.

In 1933, after 13 years of Prohibition, saloons across the United States filled up quickly when the Twenty-first Amendment legalized the sale of alcohol throughout the country.

Ida Wells-Barnett (1862-1931) used her influence as an editorial writer to speak out against mob violence and racial injustice.

3

Ida Wells-Barnett
A Fighter against Mob Violence

*A*braham Lincoln's Emancipation Proclamation, issued on New Year's Day 1863, had no immediate effect on the lives of slaves such as James and Lizzie Wells and their infant daughter, Ida, born on July 16, 1862. In early 1863, the town of Holly Springs, Mississippi, where the Wells family lived, was in Confederate hands. The family had to wait for the end of the Civil War to experience real freedom.

The Wells family led a fairly comfortable life after slavery ended. James made a good living as a carpenter and mason, and Lizzie supplemented his earnings by working as a cook. The couple bought a house, and eventually James earned enough to allow Lizzie to quit her job and become a full-time wife and mother to their seven children. The family also enjoyed educational opportunities. In 1866, a group of Methodists opened a school for former slaves in Holly Springs, where Lizzie Wells learned to read and write. (James was already literate.) The couple's oldest daughter, Ida, completed high school there and was taking college courses when tragedy struck the Wells family.

In 1878, a yellow fever epidemic in Holly Springs killed James and Lizzie Wells and their nine-month-old son. Ida was only 16 at the time—too young to be responsible for five remaining younger brothers and sisters. Three of her siblings went to live with an aunt on a farm near Holly Springs.

After passing a teachers' examination, Ida Wells got a job teaching in a rural school six miles from Holly Springs to support her family. She and her two youngest sisters later moved to Memphis, Tennessee, to live with another aunt. When she arrived in Memphis, Ida Wells first taught school in the nearby town of Woodstock. Then, in the autumn of 1884, she got a job teaching first grade in one of Memphis's schools for black children.

When Wells came to Memphis, she had no intention of stirring up trouble. She strongly believed in thrift, hard work, and individual responsibility—values she had learned at home and in school. But she was also independent, outspoken, and willing to stand up for her rights. She had no memories of slavery, when blacks had almost no rights under the law. During at least part of her childhood, blacks in Mississippi had equal access with whites to public facilities such as railroads. Moreover, black men could vote, and several of them held public office in that state. By the time Wells moved to Memphis, however, the political climate was changing. The changes prompted the young teacher to engage in the first of many protests that would characterize her life.

After the Civil War, several southern states, including Tennessee, passed laws requiring blacks to use segregated public facilities. In 1875, Congress passed the Civil Rights Act, which forbade public facilities such as hotels, restaurants, and transportation systems from discriminating against black customers.

The U.S. Supreme Court soon struck down the 1875 act. The Court's 1883 decision in *Civil Rights Cases* held that Congress had no power to impose such restrictions on private businesses. In the Court's opinion, Congress's power to enforce the Fourteenth Amendment's equal protection clause, which prohibited states from denying any person equal protection under the law, applied only to the actions of states. This meant that blacks who believed private firms had discriminated against them had to rely on the states, not the federal government, for remedies.

In May 1884, Wells boarded a train for a trip from Memphis to Woodstock. Since she had bought a first-class ticket, she sat in the women's first-class coach. When the conductor ordered her to move to the smoking car (the only car available for blacks), she resisted. A struggle followed, and Wells left the train.

On her return to Memphis, Wells sued the railroad for failing to honor her first-class ticket. Her lawsuit was the first challenge to a state segregation law after the Supreme Court decision in *Civil Rights Cases*. She won in the Tennessee lower court, but the Tennessee Supreme Court reversed the decision in 1887. The court held that by providing separate cars for black passengers, the railroad had met Tennessee's requirement that "like accommodations" be provided for blacks and whites. Because of the U.S. Supreme Court's 1883 decision, Wells had no further legal remedies.

The train incident prompted Wells to become a newspaper reporter. In the first of her many newspaper articles under the pen name "Iola," she reported her experience with Tennessee's segregated railroad facilities. In 1889, she became editor and part owner of a Memphis religious weekly, the *Free Speech and Headlight*. Her editorials for that paper became increasingly militant and cost Wells her teaching job. After she criticized the Memphis school system for providing black children with an inferior education, the school authorities refused to renew her teaching contract. Wells then decided to work full time at the newspaper.

An 1892 lynching prompted Wells to begin a life-long crusade against this crime. A lynching occurs when a mob kills someone suspected of a crime before the suspect can stand trial—often by hanging the person from a tree. The term *lynching* may have been derived from an eighteenth-century Virginia planter named Charles Lynch, who set up an illegal "court" to punish accused criminals.

Mob violence, much of it directed against blacks, occurred frequently in the South in the years following the Civil War. After 1877, when President Rutherford B. Hayes ordered the withdrawal of the last federal troops from the South, the violence increased in frequency and

President Rutherford B. Hayes (1822-1893) inadvertently put southern blacks in danger of violence by angry whites when he ordered the last federal troops out of the South in 1877.

brutality, particularly against blacks whom people believed had committed crimes against whites. Lynch mobs often dragged these suspects from their jail cells, then tortured and then killed them before they were brought to trial. For the most part, the white law enforcement agencies did nothing to discourage such lawless behavior.

The event that spurred Wells's crusade occurred in March 1892, when a mob lynched three Memphis men. The three black men had opened a grocery store in a black section of the city. The competition between the new store and a white-owned business led to a violent scuffle between blacks and whites. Afterward, a local grand jury indicted the three black businessmen for maintaining a public nuisance, and nine deputy sheriffs in civilian clothes went to the store to arrest its owners. Thinking the sheriffs were part of a lynch mob, some black residents opened fire, wounding three of the law men. The police then jailed more that two dozen blacks, including the store owners. Despite the effort of a black state militia unit that tried to protect the prisoners, a white mob lynched the three black businessmen.

The lynching infuriated Wells, who wrote a blistering editorial that urged blacks to leave the city that had refused to protect their lives and property. She also encouraged blacks to boycott the city's new streetcars because the streetcar managers said that blacks "owed" them business. Many blacks followed her advice. The resulting exodus and boycott hurt the city economically.

Wells's angry outbursts reached their peak in an 1892 editorial in which she suggested that white women had consented in many of the so-called rapes for which white mobs had lynched black men.

Now the fiery journalist was considered a real troublemaker by many white citizens. In attacking the morality of white southern women, she struck at the heart of white southern fears regarding black men. For years, southern whites had depicted black men as lustful animals, unable or unwilling to control their sexual appetites. White men justified lynchings as ways of protecting white women from black men.

However, sexual relations between white men and black women had been common in the South since the days of slavery. Wells herself, whose father was the son of a black slave and her white owner, was living proof of the practice of interracial relations in the South. But the white community drew the line at sexual relations between a black man and a white woman. Unable (or unwilling) to understand that a white woman might find a black man attractive, whites in the South regarded all such encounters as rape.

Whites reacted swiftly and violently to Wells's accusation. A mob destroyed the presses of the *Free Speech* newspaper and warned its editor, who was in New York at the time, not to return to Memphis. Wells heeded the warning and accepted a job with a New York black newspaper, the *New York Age*. There she began to investigate

MONTROSE LIBRARY DISTRICT
434 South First Street
Montrose, Colorado 81401

SOUTHERN HORRORS.

LYNCH LAW

IN ALL

ITS PHASES

Miss IDA B. WELLS,

Price, · · · Fifteen Cents.

THE NEW YORK AGE PRINT,
1892.

After a mob destroyed the presses of Free Speech
and Headlight, *Ida Wells continued writing against
mob violence as editor of* New York Age.

what people thought about lynchings and its causes. She discovered that most white people thought that the black men being lynched had raped white women and, therefore, deserved to be hanged from a tree. But most of the lynched men, in fact, had not committed rape.

Wells's articles, based on reports published in newspapers, proved that only a small percentage of black victims of lynchings had been formally accused of raping white women. The courts never had a chance to decide whether these men were guilty because mobs had lynched them before they could stand trial. Armed with these statistics, she argued that lynching was a crime motivated by greed or a desire to hold onto political power rather than a crime of moral outrage over the rape of white women. In her opinion, lynchings were part of an organized effort to keep black Americans in a subordinate position so that the white majority could exploit them economically.

In 1893, Wells moved to Chicago, where she worked for the city's first black newspaper, the *Chicago Conservator*. Two years later, she married the paper's founder, Ferdinand L. Barnett, a widower with two sons. Although she cut down on her protests during the next few years, while her two stepsons and the four children she had with Ferdinand were growing up, she never completely abandoned her crusade against lynching. During this period, Ida Wells-Barnett (as she now called herself)

Ida Wells-Barnett (left) with her husband, Ferdinand, and daughter, Alfreda

personally investigated many lynchings and wrote numerous articles and pamphlets on the subject.

Wells-Barnett's crusade against lynching often pitted her against blacks as well as whites. Black leaders such as Booker T. Washington believed their race would benefit more by trying to see things from a white person's point of view. Wells-Barnett never accepted this line of reasoning. She believed that trying to pacify whites would only make matters worse.

In 1909, Wells-Barnett joined about 60 people in calling for a conference to discuss the problem of racial violence. The meeting in New York resulted in the formation of the National Association for the Advancement of Colored People (NAACP). One of the NAACP's first projects was a national drive to end lynching. Although Wells-Barnett didn't take an active part in the campaign, the NAACP adopted many of her suggestions, such as a publicity campaign to increase public awareness of the problem and efforts to persuade Congress to make lynching a federal crime.

The NAACP's efforts were only partly successful. The group persuaded several members of Congress to introduce anti-lynching bills, but none of the bills became law. Gradually, however, due at least in part to the NAACP's publicity campaign, public opinion condemned lynching, and the wave of mob violence eventually subsided.

Educator and public speaker Booker T. Washington
(1856-1915) believed that blacks had to achieve
financial equality with whites before expecting
social equality.

The anti-lynching crusade wasn't Wells-Barnett's only reform effort. In 1913, she organized Chicago's Alpha Suffrage Club (the first black women's suffrage organization in Illinois) and took part in later campaigns for women's suffrage. Her reasoning in pushing for voting rights for women was similar to that of abolitionist Abby Kelley Foster immediately after the Civil War. Foster believed that black men needed voting rights to protect themselves against racial injustice, and Wells-Barnett believed that the right to vote was the only effective tool black Americans of both sexes had for protecting themselves against unjust laws.

Wells-Barnett was also strongly interested in electoral politics. In 1896, she campaigned for Republican presidential candidate William McKinley and took her infant son along on her statewide campaign tour. She wasn't a die-hard Republican, however. She had previously supported the candidacy of Grover Cleveland, and she later supported another Democrat, Woodrow Wilson, for the presidency.

Despite her interest in politics, Ida Wells-Barnett ran for public office only once. In 1930, when she was in her late sixties, she ran for the Illinois Senate as an independent candidate. However, she lost the election by a wide margin.

Wells-Barnett died on March 25, 1931, a few months shy of her 70th birthday. After her death, another well-known black leader, W. E. B. Du Bois, praised her as

W.E.B. Du Bois (1868-1963) founded the National Association for the Advancement of Colored People in 1909.

"the pioneer of the anti-lynching crusade in the United States . . . [who] began the awakening of the conscience of the nation." For many years, this reformer was virtually alone in her crusade. Her daughter, Alfreda, said that Wells-Barnett "fought a lonely and almost single-handed fight, with the single-mindedness of a crusader," long before others entered the fight against mob violence.

Carrie Chapman Catt (1859-1947), a leader in the fight for women's suffrage, helped to pave the way for many women who would later take part in politics.

4

Carrie Chapman Catt
Getting the Right to Vote

*O*ne autumn day in 1922, an elderly widow wrote a gently scolding letter to a close friend. Carrie Chapman Catt told her friend and longtime admirer, Mary Gray Peck, "I do wish you would stop calling me 'great.' I am the commonest old toad the Lord ever made."

Carrie Catt was too modest. Largely through her efforts, American women had finally won the right to vote on an equal basis with men. On August 27, 1920, after the Nineteenth Amendment became part of the U.S. Constitution, Catt rode triumphantly to New York's

Hotel Astor to the strains of "Hail the Conquering Hero Comes." She carried a huge bouquet of blue and yellow flowers. The National American Woman Suffrage Association (NAWSA), which Catt headed, had adopted blue and yellow as its official colors. The yellow ribbon that held the flowers together bore the words, "To Mrs. Carrie Chapman Catt from the enfranchised women of the United States." The people who arranged the victory celebration that day clearly thought that the word *great* accurately described Catt.

The fight of American women for voting rights, which began in 1848 in Seneca Falls, New York, was long and bitter. The advocates of women's suffrage sometimes quarreled among themselves, and at one point two rival suffrage organizations competed for members. The women's groups suffered many defeats before the tide turned in their favor. Early women's rights leaders such as Elizabeth Cady Stanton and Susan B. Anthony didn't live to see the final victory that Carrie Chapman Catt and a second generation of suffragists wrested from reluctant male politicians.

Carrie Clinton Lane, the second of Lucius and Maria Lane's three children, was born in Ripon, Wisconsin, on February 9, 1859. When she was seven, her family moved to a farm near Charles City, Iowa. Carrie's feminist beliefs were evident by the time she entered her teens. After learning that her mother couldn't vote in the 1872 presidential election, 13-year-old Carrie

In addition to fighting for women's suffrage, Susan B. Anthony (1820-1906) worked to give women increased access to education, higher wages, and the right to control their property and finances.

complained to a neighbor boy about the unfairness of women not being allowed to vote. His laughter and off-hand reply, "Well, naturally they can't vote," provoked an angry retort from the future suffragist leader.

After finishing high school, Carrie Lane attended Iowa's state college (now Iowa State University). She graduated in 1880—the only woman in her graduating class. She hoped to become a lawyer but soon turned to teaching in Mason City, Iowa, where she later became superintendent of schools.

Carrie Lane's marriage to Leo Chapman, a local newspaper editor, on February 12, 1885, ended her teaching career. But the marriage was short-lived. Leo

Chapman died of typhoid fever in August 1886. Shortly afterward, the young widow renewed her acquaintance with George Catt, a friend from college who had become a successful civil engineer. The young couple was married on June 10, 1890.

At the time of her second marriage, Catt had already been active in the women's suffrage movement for several years. In February 1890, she was a delegate to the convention in Washington that launched NAWSA as a merger of two rival women's suffrage groups. After her marriage, Catt, whose husband supported her efforts, continued her work as a speaker and organizer for the new group. When the aged Susan B. Anthony stepped down as NAWSA's president in 1900, Catt became president and held that office for the next four years.

In 1904, worried about the health of her husband and her mother, Catt resigned as NAWSA's president. The next few years were traumatic for Catt. Her husband died in October 1905 after an emergency operation. Her younger brother died in September 1907, and her mother died that December. To add to her troubles, Catt's own health was poor during that period. However, she remained active in both the International Woman Suffrage Alliance, which she helped to organize in 1902, and in the women's suffrage drive in New York, where she and her husband had lived for some years before his death. Catt was anxious to win the vote for women in New York because she believed that a victory in the nation's most populous state would generate enough momentum to carry the vote in other states.

The year 1915 was crucial for the suffragists. Four states, including New York, voted on women's suffrage that year. The voters—all men—defeated the measures in all four states. Shortly afterward, Dr. Anna Howard Shaw, who had succeeded Catt as president of NAWSA, resigned, and Catt reluctantly agreed to head the organization once again.

Catt's work was cut out for her, though, because the NAWSA was in a shambles. Although Shaw was an effective speaker, she had been a poor administrator. The NAWSA's treasury was depleted, morale was low, and the organization had no clear plan for winning the vote. Moreover, Alice Paul and other women frustrated with the NAWSA were challenging the organization's leadership. Paul thought the NAWSA's practice of campaigning in individual states was not a fast enough way to win women's suffrage. Instead, she favored seeking a constitutional amendment.

Paul engaged in militant demonstrations as a way of calling attention to the women's suffrage movement. She also wanted to hold the party in the White House (in this case, the Democrats) responsible for any failure to gain voting rights for women. Catt, too, favored a constitutional amendment, but she didn't want to abandon the state campaigns. Catt also disagreed with Paul's militant tactics because she believed they did more harm

Both Dr. Anna Howard Shaw (left) and Carrie Chapman Catt served as president of the National American Woman Suffrage Association (NAWSA).

than good. Moreover, Catt, who favored a nonpartisan approach, opposed any actions that would antagonize Democrats who supported women's suffrage.

On taking over as NAWSA's president, Catt immediately set out to restore the organization to good health. During the first half of 1916, she visited as many local chapters as possible. She also planned a lobbying campaign during the Republican and Democratic national conventions that summer. Because 1916 was a presidential election year, Catt hoped to get women's suffrage onto both party platforms.

Despite resistance from other suffragists, Carrie Chapman Catt believed that women could achieve their political goals within the two-party system.

Both parties responded to the NAWSA's efforts with meaningless platitudes that boiled down to one thing: Each state should decide for itself whether to let women vote. Faced with the prospect of a lengthy state-by-state fight, an infuriated Catt called an emergency convention in September 1916 to decide on the NAWSA's future strategy. When the group met, she convinced the delegates that the time had come for an all-out campaign to bring the vote to women across the nation.

Catt's "Winning Plan" called for a two-pronged effort for lobbying members of the state and federal governments. Women would try to persuade Congress to pass a constitutional amendment guaranteeing women's right to vote. At the same time, they would lobby for voting rights in states that did not allow women to vote. Of course, all of this work would take money. Catt asked the group at the emergency convention for $1 million to finance the campaign, and she raised more than $800,000 on the spot.

One serious obstacle stood in the women's path: War had broken out in Europe in 1914. Although the voters reelected President Woodrow Wilson in 1916 largely because of his slogan, "He Kept Us Out of War," the United States drifted closer to armed conflict. When the nation ended diplomatic relations with Germany in February 1917, Catt called a meeting of the NAWSA's executive council to discuss the situation. Considering

The isolationist views of Woodrow Wilson (1856-1924) during the early years of the First World War won him the support of Carrie Chapman Catt and other pacifists.

that she had helped to start the Woman's Peace Party in 1915, the thought of entering the war disturbed Catt. Although she strongly opposed war, Catt still believed that the NAWSA shouldn't jeopardize the suffrage battle by taking what was almost sure to be a futile stand against U.S. entry into the war. The meeting resulted in the NAWSA's public pledge of support for the government if war came, and it proved to be a winning decision.

For the suffragists, the war turned out to be an opportunity instead of an obstacle. During the war, Catt continued her efforts to win the vote for women, while calling attention to the importance of women's

Carrie Chapman Catt (in white, front row) leads a group of activists in a 1917 parade to boost support for women's suffrage.

contributions to the war effort and warning that under the circumstances, depriving them of the vote might be unwise. Catt took advantage of Wilson's idealistic statements that the war was being fought on behalf of democracy. She argued that the best way to teach other countries about democracy was to practice it at home by giving women the right to vote.

By the time the war ended in November 1918, victory for women's suffrage was in sight. Not only had women demonstrated their ability to handle jobs previously reserved for men, but the loyal support most of them had shown in a time of crisis also seemed to merit a reward in the form of voting rights. In addition, Alice Paul's militant tactics helped to wear down Wilson's resistance to endorsing woman suffrage. Paul and her National Woman's Party, which she had formed in 1916, started picketing the White House.

In January 1918, President Wilson asked members of the House of Representatives to support a constitutional amendment giving women the right to vote. The House passed the amendment, but it stalled in the Senate. Clearly, the women would have to wait a little longer to win the right to vote.

As her goal of women's suffrage grew closer, Catt thought about how women would use their new right. Many of them had little or no experience with politics. So, during the NAWSA's Jubilee Convention in March 1919, which celebrated the 50th anniversary of the

In her fight for women's suffrage, Alice Paul (1885-1977) once chained herself to the White House fence.

founding of the rival National and American Woman Suffrage Associations, Catt laid the groundwork for the new League of Women Voters, which was to to replace the NAWSA after women had won the right to vote.

Soon after it was formed, the League began promoting education in responsible citizenship. Although the League took a stand on political issues, it didn't endorse political parties or individual candidates. Catt, however, encouraged women to join the League and become active in the political party of their choice. She believed that the real struggle for women to become fully active in politics would be won on the inside of political parties. After organizing the League, Catt left its operation in the hands of younger women and accepted the post of honorary chair.

Meanwhile, the suffragists geared up for one last push for a constitutional amendment. During a special session of the new Sixty-sixth Congress in the spring of 1919, both houses passed the amendment. Then the battle for state ratification began. One by one, the states agreed to the amendment, until Tennessee's ratification put the amendment over the top in August 1920.

Carrie Chapman Catt's political skills were largely responsible for this victory. She understood that politicians were not likely to agree to demands for sweeping reforms unless most citizens were in favor of such changes. Catt therefore refrained from endorsing radical reforms of American society. She also avoided confrontational tactics such as picketing. Instead, she focused on the goal of achieving voting rights for women by using traditional political methods: firm leadership, a coherent and logical game plan, calm, well-reasoned arguments, and a strong grassroots organization. She recognized the importance of compromise as a political tool and was willing to make political compromises when necessary. Her moderate ways had led to success.

Women had campaigned for the right to vote since the mid-1800s, but the Nineteenth Amendment granting women's suffrage did not pass until August 1920.

*An early meeting of the League of Women Voters,
which was formed in 1920*

Catt claimed to despise politicians and once said
that politics was "no place for a reformer." However, in
1919 a journalist described Catt as "a professional woman
politician." He was essentially correct.

Catt spent most of her later years working for world
peace. She strongly supported the League of Nations
that formed after World War I, and she was bitterly dis-
appointed when the United States failed to join the new
organization. Still, she continued to work with women

Even after women won the right to vote, Carrie Chapman Catt knew there were more inequities that needed to be changed.

throughout the world in support of peaceful solutions to international disagreements. In her opinion, war was a relic of barbarism that nations of the world should have abolished long ago.

In 1925, Catt organized the Committee on the Cause and Cure of War and served as its president until 1932. Despite the outbreak of World War II in Europe in 1939, the group continued to meet until the end of 1940. It disbanded in 1943, two years after the United States had entered the war, and a successor organization—the Women's Action Committee for Victory and Lasting Peace—began holding meetings that same year. Catt supported the new organization, which she hoped would preach that war was immoral. She believed that civilization could be saved only by adopting such a firm policy.

Carrie Chapman Catt lived to see both the end of World War II in 1945 and the first meeting of the United Nations, a new vehicle for world peace, in 1946. She died on March 9, 1947. A longtime personal friend, commenting on Catt's death in the *The Nation* magazine, praised her 60 years of work to achieve equality for women and develop a peaceful means for international change. In the writer's opinion, Catt was not only "a great human being" but also a political thinker of the first order.

After women won the right to vote, Molly Dewson (1874-1962) spent her career trying to get women more actively involved in the political process.

5

Molly Dewson
A Political Boss

*L*ate in the summer of 1928, a middle-aged woman received an urgent telephone call that thrust her overnight into the world of presidential politics. The caller wanted her to handle a problem that had come up in St. Louis during Governor Alfred E. Smith's campaign for the presidency. Someone had to head off a potentially damaging squabble between two rival Democratic women. Even though she had no experience with presidential election campaigns, Molly Dewson quickly agreed. It was hard to turn down her friend Eleanor Roosevelt.

*Long-time friends Eleanor Roosevelt (right) and
Molly Dewson attend a political dinner at the
Mayflower Hotel in Washington, D.C.*

Eleanor Roosevelt, who would soon become the First Lady of the United States, was handling the women's division of the Smith campaign. She believed that Molly Dewson was the right person for the job. Within a few days, Dewson solved the problem by sending both women on the campaign trail—in different directions. The trip began a new phase in Dewson's life. At age 54, the energetic New Englander whose foghorn voice, "mannish" clothes, and forthright manner earned her the nicknames "Queen Molly," "The Colonel," and "The General," was on the verge of a career as one of the country's first female political bosses, outclassed only by Eleanor Roosevelt's own political genius.

Mary Williams Dewson came from a town steeped in American history. The youngest of Edward and Elizabeth Dewson's six children, she was born in Quincy, Massachusetts, on February 18, 1874. As a child, she often saw the aged Charles Francis Adams, a Civil War diplomat whose father and grandfather were both United States presidents, walking in his garden. But the Dewson family had its own connection with American history. Molly's great-great-grandfather took part in the Boston Tea Party in 1773, an early step in the American colonists' fight for independence from England.

While growing up, Molly (as she preferred to be called) scorned girls games and toys, preferring to roam outdoors or play with her army of paper soldiers. She also pitched on a boys softball team. As she grew older, she

Molly Dewson and Betsy Roosevelt (Franklin and Eleanor Roosevelt's daughter-in-law), attend a 1938 party sponsored by the the Women's National Press Club.

never seemed interested in boys or dating. Her ambition was to attend college.

Dewson got her first taste of politics at nearby Wellesley College, which she entered in the autumn of 1893. She was interested in government throughout her four years at the women's college. During her sophomore and senior years, her classmates elected her class president. In a fictional flashback from the future, the 1897 Wellesley yearbook reminded readers that the campaign electing Dewson as the United States president was "one of the glories of American history."

After graduation, Dewson took a job as a research assistant for the Women's Educational and Industrial Union in Boston. She needed the money because her father was very ill, which put a severe strain on the family's finances. (Edward Dewson died in 1898.) Molly Dewson's first assignment for the union was to study why young women often preferred factory jobs to domestic work. This assignment gave Dewson an opportunity to use the analytical skills she had acquired in college and continued to use throughout her career.

In 1900, Dewson took a job as the probation officer for the Massachusetts State Industrial School for Girls, the nation's first girls reform school. In 1904, she became the school's superintendent of probation and parole, a job she held until 1912. This job was important to Dewson's personal as well as professional life. In 1909, a young social worker named Mary "Polly" Porter signed up for some practical experience with the probation agency. Porter and her supervisor, Molly Dewson, soon became friends. Their friendship lasted more than half a century.

In 1911, Dewson took a leave of absence from her parole work to help with a study of the need for a minimum wage for women workers in Massachusetts. Working at a breakneck pace to meet the legislature's January 1912 deadline for presenting the report, the group showed that many of the state's working women were barely able to survive on their earnings. As a result of the report, the legislature created a permanent commission to establish minimum pay levels for women in various industries. Dewson turned down an offer to become the commission's executive secretary because she was needed at home to help her mother, who was very ill.

After her mother's death in December 1912, Dewson and Porter bought a dairy farm near Worcester, Massachusetts, and settled down as "gentlewoman farmers." (They hired people to do the actual farm work.) At that time, it was fairly common for two well-educated single women to live together. The living arrangement, called a "Boston marriage," was a socially acceptable alternative to living with one's family. (Living alone wasn't considered respectable for a middle-class woman.) If there were hints of a sexual side to the relationship, people closed their eyes or looked the other way.

Whatever their sexual orientation, the Porter-Dewsons, as the two women called themselves, were a good match. They clearly cared deeply about one another and were seldom separated for any length of time after they began sharing living quarters in the spring of 1913.

In 1915, the two "partners" (their term for one another) volunteered to help the Massachusetts Woman Suffrage Association in its campaign for approval of the state referendum on voting rights for women. The two women soon became a familiar sight in Worcester County, as they cruised around in an automobile decorated with suffrage banners. The referendum lost overwhelmingly, but it pushed Dewson to the forefront of the women's suffrage movement in Massachusetts. She and Porter were both delegates to the 1915 National American Woman Suffrage Association's convention when Carrie Chapman Catt assumed the organization's presidency for a second time. In 1916, Dewson became head of the Massachusetts Woman Suffrage Association's legislative committee.

The advent of World War I ended the couple's suffragist activities. In the autumn of 1917, they signed up for duty in France as Red Cross volunteers. Dewson advanced quickly in the Red Cross ranks. By the war's end, she was in charge of relief work in the entire southern third of France. After the war, the Red Cross asked both women to stay on in France, but they decided to return to the United States instead.

Not long after her return from France, Dewson accepted a job as research secretary for a reform organization called the National Consumers' League. In her new job, Dewson concentrated on the minimum wage issue that she had worked on in 1911. For three years she worked almost full time assisting a Harvard Law School professor, Felix Frankfurter, prepare legal briefs defending a District of Columbia minimum wage law for women and children. (Children often held paying jobs during this period of history.)

Dewson's efforts earned her the nickname "Minimum Wage Dewson." Although they met with initial success, the law's defenders lost the final battle when, in 1923, the U.S. Supreme Court struck down the law, saying it was an infringement on workers' and employers' freedom of contract. Dewson and the Harvard professor had the last word on the minimum wage issue, however. In 1940, Frankfurter, who had become an associate justice on the Supreme Court in 1939, participated in the Court's unanimous decision in *U.S. v. Darby*. In the decision, the Court upheld the Fair Labor Standards Act, which contained a minimum wage provision.

In 1924, Dewson resigned from her job with the National Consumers' League to become civic secretary for the Women's City Club of New York. Although she stayed in the new job less than a year, it influenced her later career. During that time, she met the club's new vice-president, Eleanor Roosevelt, and her husband,

Franklin Delano Roosevelt (whom many people referred to by his initials, FDR).

In the autumn of 1925, Dewson left her job at the Women's City Club to begin a four-month tour of Italy and Africa with Porter. On her return, she spent her time lobbying the state legislature on behalf of various reforms and enjoying summer vacations at Porter's home in Castine, Maine. While at the Maine house in 1928, Dewson got the telephone call from Eleanor Roosevelt that propelled her into national Democratic politics.

In 1939, nearly 20 years after working with Molly Dewson, Felix Frankfurter, (1882-1965) was appointed to the U.S. Supreme Court.

While Dewson was busy with the 1928 presidential campaign, FDR was running a successful campaign for governor of New York. In 1930, Eleanor Roosevelt drafted Dewson to help with his reelection campaign. Dewson accepted the offer and worked under the general direction of James Farley, who had managed Franklin Roosevelt's 1928 campaign. (Dewson and Farley would be colleagues again in the future. Farley later became FDR's postmaster general and head of the Democratic National Committee.)

FDR's landslide victory in 1930 in the New York governor's race made him a front-runner for his party's nomination in the 1932 presidential election. Dewson was a close friend of the Roosevelts by that time and was part of the small group of people that pushed FDR's candidacy for more than a year before the 1932 national convention.

After FDR's nomination, Dewson headed the Women's Division of the Democratic National Campaign Committee, where she introduced a number of innovative ideas for getting women involved at the grassroots level. One particularly successful idea was the distribution of one-page fact sheets printed on colored paper. These sheets were color-coded, with a different color for each topic. Dewson's group distributed several million of these "Rainbow Fliers" to women campaign workers for use in house-to-house canvassing.

Eight hundred Democrats, including Franklin D.
Roosevelt (center), attend a dinner to honor Molly
Dewson on December 16, 1932.

Uninterested in personal recognition, Dewson preferred a behind-the-scenes role. After FDR's 1932 presidential election and with Eleanor Roosevelt's help,
Dewson quietly pushed for the appointment of as many
qualified women as possible to high-level government
posts. Her efforts earned her a new nickname, "More
Women Dewson."

The business of getting men to appoint women to political positions was far from easy. In one instance, Dewson commented, "I had to fight for it like a bag of cats." Her good-natured persistence often paid off, however. Her trophies included a few "firsts" for women: Frances Perkins as secretary of labor (the first woman Cabinet member), former U.S. Representative Ruth Bryan Owen of Florida as American minister to Denmark (the first woman to represent the United States in a foreign country), and Florence Allen as a U.S. Court of Appeals judge (the first woman appointed to a federal appeals court). Dewson was unsuccessful, however, in getting FDR to nominate Florence Allen to fill one of the several vacancies on the U.S. Supreme Court that arose during Roosevelt's time in office.

Dewson didn't carry out all her political work behind the scenes, however. In 1933, the Democrats rewarded her for her campaign help by giving her a full-time salaried job as director of the Women's Division of the Democratic National Committee. The job required her to commute between Washington, D.C., and New York City, where she and Porter shared an apartment. The strain proved to be too much for her. In 1934, she quit the paying job and became an unpaid adviser in the committee's New York office.

Dewson also held three formal advisory positions during the Roosevelt administration. She served on the Consumers' Advisory Board and the Advisory Council to

Frances Perkins (1882-1965), the first woman appointed to the U.S. cabinet, served as the secretary of labor from 1933 to 1945.

*Eleanor Roosevelt (right) watches as James Farley
congratulates Molly Dewson on her appointment as
head of the Democratic National Committee's
Women's Division.*

the Committee on Economic Security, which helped to develop the 1935 Social Security Act. In 1937, she became a member of the Social Security Board, which oversaw the administration of the 1935 law, but left the position in 1938 due to poor health.

In 1936, Dewson again headed the Women's Division of the Democratic National Committee. During that year's national convention, she persuaded party leaders to adopt a new rule whereby each state's Democratic organization would appoint a member and an alternate (one male and one female) to the party's national platform committee. At the convention, the women alternates (who attended every meeting their male counterparts didn't attend) managed to insert a few general statements of interest to women into the party platform. They didn't succeed in including any specific proposals, however.

After the Democrats' landslide victory in the 1936 election, Dewson again gave up her position as head of the party's women's division. Shortly after FDR's second inauguration in March 1937, Eleanor Roosevelt and Postmaster General James Farley organized a "Molly Dewson Round Up" in recognition of Dewson's work for the party. In a gesture reminiscent of her college classmates' 1897 yearbook "flashback" to "President Molly Dewson," the group of Democrats playfully nominated Dewson to run for president in 1940. At that time, FDR's controversial bid for a third term was far in the future. When President Roosevelt ran for reelection in 1940, Dewson came out of retirement to help her good friend once more.

In 1960, Dewson, who had lived with Polly Porter in Castine, Maine, since 1952, ran for elective office for the first and only time when she agreed to be a Democratic candidate for the Maine Senate. The gesture was purely symbolic, though. Hancock County, where Dewson and

During his 12 years as U.S. president, Franklin D. Roosevelt (1882-1945) established several new government agencies and became the first president to appoint a woman to the cabinet.

Porter lived, had never elected a Democrat to that office. Dewson lost by an overwhelming margin.

The 1960 effort was Dewson's last try in politics. On October 17, 1962, she suffered a stroke at the Porter-Dewson home. The woman that one Roosevelt administration official called "the greatest politician in our gang" died four days later. A little more than two weeks afterward, her friend Eleanor Roosevelt also died, and an era in American women's history came to an end.

Civil rights leader Pauli Murray (1910-1985) used the courtroom as a battlefield for ending discrimination.

6

Pauli Murray
Ahead of the Crowd

*D*uring the 1956 Democratic National Convention, Eleanor Roosevelt cautioned civil rights advocates against pushing too hard in the upcoming presidential election campaign for vigorous enforcement of the U.S. Supreme Court's recent decision that outlawed racial segregation in public schools. Instead, the former First Lady advised the civil rights leaders to adopt a moderate stance on this politically sensitive issue. Although her advice was a politically sound rule of thumb—politicians can't afford to move too far ahead of the voters if they hope to get elected—in this instance, many black Democrats disagreed with her. They wanted segregation to end as soon as possible.

Eleanor Roosevelt's friend, Pauli Murray, was among those who disagreed with the former First Lady. A descendent of black slaves and white slave owners, Murray had always been several steps ahead of the crowd in the struggle to achieve equal justice for all Americans.

Anna Pauline Murray, the fourth of William and Agnes Murray's six children, was born in Baltimore, Maryland, on November 20, 1910. Will Murray taught in the city's segregated schools, and Agnes Fitzgerald Murray, a North Carolina native, had graduated from a nurses' training school. Shortly after their marriage, Will became seriously ill with typhoid fever. He recovered with the help of his wife's nursing skills, but he soon began having recurring spells of depression, alternating with unpredictable violent moods. The couple frequently separated, then reconciled soon afterward. But the family's life was permanently disrupted in March 1914, when Agnes Murray died from a cerebral hemorrhage, leaving six children ranging in age from nine years to six months.

After Agnes Murray's death, Will's sister and younger brother, who lived nearby, took the two youngest children to live with them, and Agnes's sister Pauline took three-year-old Pauli to Durham, North Carolina, to live with the Fitzgeralds. Will Murray kept the three oldest children with him for a time, but his mental condition continued to deteriorate. He was eventually committed to a state mental hospital, where he died in 1923 after a savage beating from a white hospital attendant. This crime shocked and angered young Pauli, and it eventually helped lead her to a lifelong battle for racial justice.

Despite the tragic circumstances that had brought about the move to North Carolina, the new location was good for Pauli. Her Fitzgerald relatives gave her both a stable, middle-class environment and a strong religious faith. Her grandmother and her aunts Pauline and Sallie were all devout members of the Episcopal church. The Fitzgeralds also taught Pauli to take pride in her racial ancestry, which included blacks, whites, and Native Americans.

Pauli's grandmother, Cornelia Smith Fitzgerald, was the offspring of a white lawyer, Sidney Smith, and his family's part-black, part-Cherokee slave, Harriet. Pauli's grandfather, Robert Fitzgerald, the son of a free black Pennsylvania farmer and his white wife, fought for the Union during the Civil War. After the war, he had settled in North Carolina, where he married Cornelia Smith and helped her to raise their six children. This heritage helped Pauli to see things from more than one point of view during her later struggles for racial justice.

After graduating in 1926 from Durham's all-black high school—which only taught through the 11th grade—Pauli lived with a cousin in New York while attending Hunter College, one of the city's tuition-free

*Growing up in the segregated South, Pauli Murray
learned about racial discrimination firsthand.*

public colleges. Before starting classes, though, she had to take a final year of high school to meet the college's demanding admission standards. She then worked for a year to pay for the cost of books and other college supplies. Pauli graduated from Hunter in January 1933 and was one of four black graduates in a class of 247.

During the 1930s and 1940s—years before the civil-rights movement received national attention—Murray challenged racial segregation in higher education, public transportation, and public eating places. Although she met with little immediate success, her efforts paved the way for later reformers in the 1950s and 1960s who forced the South to end racially segregated public facilities.

In 1938, Murray applied for admission to the all-white University of North Carolina's graduate school in Chapel Hill, which was near her relatives' home in Durham. At that time, there were no public graduate schools for black students in North Carolina. Although the school had never admitted a black student, a 1938 Supreme Court decision seemed to apply in her case. In *Gaines v. Canada*, the Court ruled that the state of Missouri, which had no public law school for black residents, had either to provide blacks with a legal education that was substantially equal to what it provided for its white residents or admit them to the white law school.

After the University of North Carolina refused to admit her, Murray asked the National Association for the Advancement of Colored People for help, citing the

Missouri case. The NAACP's young assistant counsel, Thurgood Marshall, declined to file a lawsuit on her behalf because he wanted a court case that would clearly rest on constitutional grounds. Thurgood Marshall felt that because Murray had lived in New York for so many years, the North Carolina university might argue that its refusal to admit her was due to her nonresident status and not her race. Murray, who couldn't afford to pay a lawyer's fees, lost her 1938 bid for admission to the University of North Carolina. (In 1951, however, in response to a federal court order in another case, the school finally opened its doors to black students.)

In 1967, civil rights attorney Thurgood Marshall (1908-1993) became the first African American appointed to the U.S. Supreme Court.

Pauli Murray realized she could help put an end to racial discrimination by studying the desegregation rulings decided from within the walls of the U.S. Supreme Court.

Two years later, in 1940, Murray tested the South's practice of racial segregation on interstate buses. She and a friend were traveling by bus from Washington, D.C., to Durham. While the bus was traveling through Virginia (which required blacks to occupy the rear seats on public transportation), Murray and her friend tried to move to seats near the front. After an argument with the driver, the two were arrested and spent the weekend in jail. A local court later found them guilty of disturbing the peace.

Although Murray's tactics didn't work in 1940, in 1946 the Supreme Court held in *Morgan v. Virginia* that the Virginia law requiring segregation on buses that crossed state lines was unconstitutional. Despite the Court's ruling, it wasn't until the 1960s that civil rights activists succeeded in desegregating interstate buses throughout the South.

In the autumn of 1941, Murray enrolled in Howard University Law School in Washington, D.C. (Howard University, founded in 1867, is one of the oldest black colleges in the United States.) Before long, she was again protesting racial segregation—this time in Washington's public eating places. In April 1943, Murray and about 20 other Howard University students desegregated a cafeteria in a black section of the city. After the cafeteria employees refused to serve the black students, they quietly occupied all the available seats in the restaurant. Faced with a loss of business, the owner quickly gave in and ordered his employees to begin serving both black and white customers.

When the students tried the same tactics in a downtown Washington cafeteria the following year, the university officials, fearing a loss of the school's federal funds (which made up about half of Howard's budget), ordered them to stop the demonstrations. The students reluctantly obeyed. In the early 1960s, however, civil rights groups used similar tactics to desegregate public eating places in many parts of the South.

During her three years at Howard, Murray examined the constitutional basis for racial segregation. In its fight to end this practice, the NAACP had challenged two nineteenth-century Supreme Court decisions that supported the states' right to impose racial segregation.

One was the *Civil Rights Cases* decision of 1883 that had prevented journalist Ida Wells from taking her dispute concerning Tennessee's segregated railroads to the federal courts. The 1896 decision of *Plessy v. Ferguson* held that states could maintain racial segregation so long as they provided equal facilities for blacks and whites.

Murray's studies convinced her that instead of arguing about the equality of segregated facilities on an individual case basis, the NAACP should try to get the Supreme Court to reverse the two earlier decisions. In her senior year at Howard University, she wrote a paper arguing that segregation harmed minorities, regardless of how good the segregated facilities might be. No one paid much attention to her argument at the time, but years later Thurgood Marshall used some of the same reasoning in successfully arguing the *Brown v. The Board of Education of Topeka* case before the Supreme Court. The Court's 1954 decision in the *Brown* case held that segregated schools were inherently unequal, and therefore violated the Fourteenth Amendment's guarantee of equal protection under the law.

It was the uproar in the South over the *Brown* decision that led Eleanor Roosevelt to advise Pauli Murray and others not to argue too strenuously for its immediate enforcement for fear of hurting the Democrats' chance of winning the 1956 presidential election. By that time, Murray and Roosevelt had become good friends. They had first met in the early 1940s, when Murray was

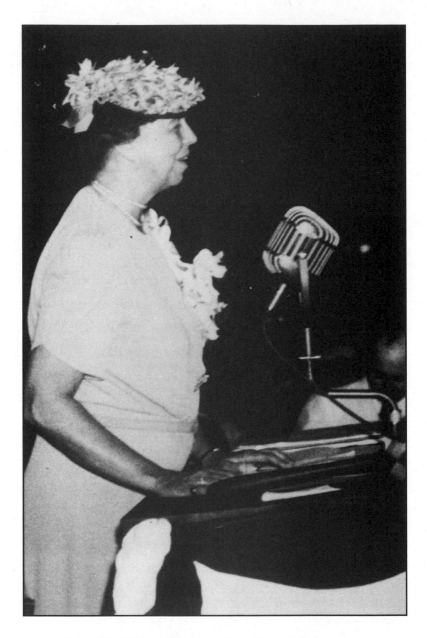

In 1940, Eleanor Roosevelt (1884-1962) became the first First Lady to speak at a national party convention.

organizing activities to help poor tenant farmers, a cause enthusiastically supported by the First Lady. Although Eleanor Roosevelt's warmth and openness charmed her, Murray frequently argued with her new friend about public issues. Roosevelt generally tried to restrain Murray's impetuous demands for instant reforms, even though she sympathized with Murray's point of view. Despite their many differences of opinion, the friendship was important in Murray's development as a fighter for racial equality.

Murray's interest in racial justice gradually led her to an awareness that gender-based discrimination was every bit as pervasive and deep-rooted as racial discrimination. She had firsthand experience with both forms of discrimination. After graduating from Howard, she applied to Harvard Law School to study for an advanced law degree. The school turned down her application, citing its longstanding policy of not admitting women. By the time Harvard Law School began to admit women in 1951, Murray had received a master's degree in law from the University of California at Berkeley.

After completing her studies in California, Murray returned to New York to practice law. During that period, she made her first and only attempt to win an elective office. In 1949, she ran unsuccessfully for a seat on New York's city council. Afterward, she worked for several years in a New York law firm and then spent about a year and a half in Ghana, where she taught law at the newly independent African country's law school. After returning from Ghana in June 1961, Murray enrolled in Yale Law School, which awarded her the degree of Doctor of Juridical Science in 1965. She was the first black student to receive this degree from Yale.

In 1962, Murray joined a committee that was working for the President's Commission on the Status of Women (PCSW), which Eleanor Roosevelt chaired until her death in November of that year. At that time, the National Woman's Party was pushing for congressional action on a constitutional amendment to guarantee equal rights for women. The Equal Rights Amendment (ERA), first introduced in Congress in 1923, had never received congressional approval.

Many women's groups opposed the ERA because they feared it would destroy legal protections women already had, such as entitlement to financial support from their husbands and not being drafted into the military. Hoping to avoid continued controversy over the ERA, the PCSW asked its Committee on Civil and Political Rights, which Murray headed, to explore other avenues for achieving equal treatment for women. Murray's analysis convinced her that the ERA wasn't needed because the Fourteenth Amendment already gave women all the protection the new amendment would give them. She recommended the development of lawsuits to test her theory in court. The PCSW adopted Murray's suggestion in its October 1963 report to President John F. Kennedy.

The President's Commission on the Status of Women report that Pauli Murray helped to write reached President John F. Kennedy's desk one month before his assassination on November 22, 1963.

As a member of the American Civil Liberties Union's Women's Rights Project, Murray worked on a series of test cases that she had recommended. As a result of the project's work, the Supreme Court issued several decisions during the 1970s that clarified women's rights. The Court generally agreed with Murray's contention that the Fourteenth Amendment's equal protection clause forbade gender-based discrimination.

In *Reed v. Reed* (1971), the first of these decisions, the Court unanimously struck down an Idaho law that gave males preference over females in the administration of deceased persons' estates, calling it arbitrary and unreasonable. Ruth Bader Ginsburg, an ACLU lawyer and future U.S. Supreme Court justice, wrote the plaintiff's brief in the *Reed* case. Ginsburg listed Murray, who was then teaching at Brandeis University, as a co-author because Murray's work in other cases paved the way for the *Reed* case.

Toward the end of her life, Murray felt that God was calling her to a religious ministry. In 1973, she gave up a tenured position at Brandeis to enter a theological

In 1993, 22 years after working on the Reed v. Reed *discrimination case, Ruth Bader Ginsburg became the second woman appointed to the U.S. Supreme Court.*

seminary. She was the only black woman in the seminary. After receiving a Master of Divinity degree in 1976, she became a deacon in the Episcopal church. At that time, the church didn't admit women to the priesthood. In this instance, Murray's timing was right. Later that year, the church decided to allow women to become priests.

In an ordination ceremony on January 8, 1977, at the National Cathedral in Washington, D.C., Murray became the first black woman in the United States to enter the Episcopal priesthood. A little over a month later, she conducted her first communion service at the chapel in North Carolina where her grandmother Cornelia had been baptized more than a century before.

Pauli Murray died on July 1, 1985. Five years later, the University of North Carolina, which had once refused to admit her as a student, created a scholarship in her honor. The Pauli Murray Scholarship rewards under-graduates who have contributed significantly to the improvement of race relations on the university's Chapel Hill campus.

Fannie Lou Hamer (1917-1977) was threatened, arrested, and beaten during her crusade against racial hatred.

7

Fannie Lou Hamer
Civil Rights Champion

One summer evening in 1962, a small group of African Americans gathered in a church in Ruleville, Mississippi, to listen to two visitors. The speakers, who represented a coalition of civil rights organizations, were asking the audience to help register black voters. Fannie Lou Hamer, then in her mid-forties, was one of the few people who volunteered to encourage blacks to register to vote. Her decision that evening brought her into the center of the civil rights movement that transformed the South in the 1960s.

Fannie Lou Townsend, the youngest of James and Lou Ella Townsend's 20 children, was born in Montgomery County, Mississippi, on October 6, 1917. When she was two years old, the family moved to Sunflower County, about 100 miles north of Jackson, where they supported themselves by working as sharecroppers. (The term *sharecropper* refers to an arrangement under which a person farms someone else's land for a share of the crop. The sharecropper often had to repay the landowner for the cost of seeds and other supplies after the crop was harvested. Moreover, sharecroppers often had to buy groceries, clothing, and other personal items on credit at the landowner's store. As a result, most sharecroppers not only lacked adequate housing, nutrition, and medical care, but also went through life in debt to the landowner.)

During Fannie Lou's childhood, conditions in Mississippi were in some ways worse for blacks, regardless of their economic circumstances, than they had been when reformer Ida Wells had left the state some 50 years earlier. Racial segregation was the norm in many areas of life, and discriminatory rules kept most blacks from voting. Lynchings, which Wells had fought so hard to stop during the early part of the century, were still common in Mississippi when Fannie Lou was growing up.

While in her late twenties, Fannie Lou Townsend married Perry Hamer, a sharecropper whom most people called "Pap." The Hamers lived in a small house on a white-owned plantation outside Ruleville. Fannie Lou cooked and cleaned for the plantation owner when she wasn't picking cotton, doing her own household chores, or caring for the Hamers' two foster children. Their lives went on in much the same way until the civil rights movement turned their world upside down.

After the end of World War II, increasing numbers of black Americans, particularly returning war veterans, rebelled against the laws and practices that kept them in a second-class status. Earlier generations of blacks had failed to gain for themselves the civil and political rights that most white Americans took for granted. This new

Laws in the segregated South often prevented blacks and whites from attending the same schools, eating at the same lunch counters, and drinking from the same water fountains.

generation of blacks vowed that this time their efforts would succeed.

The Supreme Court's 1954 decision outlawing segregation in public schools was the first crack in the wall of segregation that white southerners had erected between themselves and their black neighbors. Other cracks soon appeared. In 1955, a group of black residents of Montgomery, Alabama, organized a boycott that resulted in the desegregation of the city's buses. That action propelled one of its leaders, Dr. Martin Luther King, Jr., and his Southern Christian Leadership Conference (SCLC) into national prominence.

In 1960, a group of college students from the Student Nonviolent Coordinating Committee (SNCC) began a series of "sit-ins" at lunch counters that resulted in many white-owned restaurants in the South deciding to serve black customers. In 1961, the Congress of Racial Equality (CORE) organized "freedom rides" in which groups of whites and blacks successfully challenged racial segregation on interstate buses and in bus depots that served interstate passengers in the South.

Many civil rights leaders believed that, regardless of what other gains they might achieve, the power of the vote was essential for improving conditions for blacks in the South, where discriminatory laws often prevented blacks from voting. This goal motivated the civil rights workers who went to Mississippi in 1962 to persuade blacks to register to vote. The workers knew they had an uphill fight. Mississippi had one of the most deeply entrenched systems of segregation in the South, and Sunflower County was a stronghold of white resistance to the civil rights movement. For example, Senator James O. Eastland of Mississippi, the powerful head of the Senate Judiciary Committee, was an avowed segregationist.

On August 31, 1962, Fannie Lou Hamer and 17 others boarded a privately owned bus for the trip from Ruleville to the Sunflower County seat in Indianola to register to vote. As expected, Hamer failed the literacy test required of all potential voters. (She and other blacks were asked to explain a little-known section of the state

Senator James O. Eastland of Mississippi fought hard in Washington, D.C., to prevent desegregation in the South.

117

constitution while whites usually had to read only a few simple words.)

On the way home from Indianola, a white police officer arrested the bus driver for driving a vehicle that looked too much like a school bus. The passengers were able to scrape together enough money to pay the driver's fine. But when Hamer arrived home, the white plantation owner she worked for ordered her to leave his property. He later relented and offered to let her come back if she abandoned her effort to register to vote. But Fannie Lou Hamer refused. Instead, she stayed with friends and relatives for a short time and then went on an extended fund-raising tour for the SNCC.

Hamer proved to be a powerful grassroots advocate for the civil rights movement. This sharecropper with little formal education had an unusual ability to move audiences with her sincerity, her down-to-earth language, and her message of nonviolence. Her singing matched her powerful speaking voice. Time after time, she inspired audiences with her strong contralto that throbbed with passion as she led them in "freedom songs," familiar hymns and spirituals whose words were sometimes changed to emphasize the civil rights message.

In June 1963, Hamer (by that time a paid employee for the SNCC's voter registration campaign) attended a training session for registration workers in Charleston, South Carolina. While she and a group of fellow students were on their way home by bus, some of them tried to

During her years as a civil rights activist, Fannie Lou Hamer was known for her commanding speaking voice and strong religious convictions.

order food at a whites-only lunch counter at the bus depot in Winona, Mississippi. By that time, the Interstate Commerce Commission had responded to the freedom rides by issuing rules forbidding racial segregation in interstate transportation facilities.

These rules, however, didn't stop local police officers from arresting Hamer and five of her fellow passengers. During the group's three-day stay at the county jail, two black inmates, acting under orders from the white law enforcement officers, clubbed Hamer repeatedly with a blackjack. The incident prompted the federal government to file both civil and criminal charges against the local officials responsible for the arrest and mistreatment of the prisoners. From Hamer's viewpoint, neither action achieved justice. In December 1963, an all-white jury acquitted the white defendants, and in May 1964 the U.S. Justice Department agreed to the dismissal of its civil suit. Nevertheless, the court actions were an important early sign of the federal government's willingness to defend the civil rights of black citizens.

In the latter part of 1963, the SNCC debated the question of asking northern white college students to help with a planned voter registration drive in Mississippi the following year. Hamer, still recovering from her beating, argued in favor of getting help from anyone willing to give it—black or white. She prevailed, and the SNCC enlisted white students in the drive that became known as "Freedom Summer," a project in which Hamer played a significant role.

In the spring of 1964, Hamer went to Oxford, Ohio, to help with the orientation of the Freedom Summer volunteers. As she had done before, Hamer stressed the need for love, not hatred, in dealing with white Mississippians. There was too much hate, she reminded her young listeners. Hamer was right about the existence of hatred during that turbulent summer. Before the orientation sessions ended, three civil rights workers disappeared in Neshoba County, Mississippi. One of the missing workers was Andrew Goodman, a young Freedom Summer volunteer who had just arrived in Mississippi after completing his orientation.

The extensive search for the missing trio ended early in August, when law enforcement officers found the bodies of Goodman, James Chaney, and Michael Schwerner, by a dam near Philadelphia, Mississippi. All three had been shot at close range, and Chaney, a local black whom Schwerner had recruited for CORE, had been severely beaten. (Seven men, including a Neshoba County deputy sheriff, eventually went to federal prisons for their part in the murders.)

Before Freedom Summer began, Hamer and other civil rights workers had become convinced that they

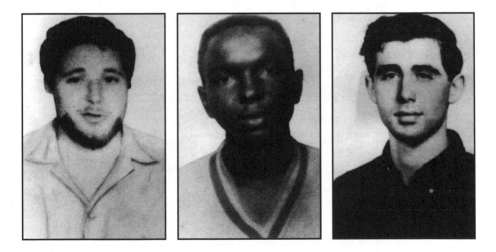

Civil rights workers (left to right) Michael Schwerner, James Chaney, and Andrew Goodman were slain during the "Freedom Summer" of 1964.

wouldn't make real progress without challenging the political power of the state's white Democratic leaders. (Mississippi was virtually a one-party state at that time.) In April 1964, Hamer was part of a group that organized the Mississippi Freedom Democratic Party (MFDP) as an alternative to the regular party organization.

Hamer was vice-chair of the 68-person MFDP delegation that went to Atlantic City, New Jersey, in August 1964 to challenge the seating of the white delegation at the Democratic National Convention. Her testimony during the televised hearings before the convention's Credentials Committee described the harassment she had endured as a result of her attempt to exercise her voting right. Hamer ended with a tearful indictment of an America that allowed such torment to happen to people whose only offense was trying to become first-class citizens.

After Hamer's testimony, support for the MFDP poured in from people all over the United States who were already shocked over the discovery of the bodies of the murdered civil rights workers. The controversy over the Mississippi delegation alarmed the Democratic leaders. Anxious to avoid a battle on the convention floor that might trigger a massive walkout by southern delegates, party leaders worked out a compromise under which two hand-picked male MFDP delegates would be seated, along with any regular Mississippi Democrats willing to pledge their loyalty to the party's nominee.

(Many of the state's regular Democrats had already expressed a preference for the Republican nominee, Senator Barry Goldwater of Arizona.)

Most civil rights leaders thought the compromise was reasonable, but not Fannie Lou Hamer. She argued loud and long against any compromise whatsoever. Many of her colleagues tried to persuade her that compromise was a valid and necessary part of political life, but Hamer disagreed. Hamer won her argument, and the MFDP rejected the offered settlement. The Credentials Committee, however, pretended that the MFDP had accepted the compromise, and the convention delegates

Although many southern Democrats supported Senator Barry Goldwater, the 1964 Republican presidential candidate lost the election to Democrat Lyndon B. Johnson.

adopted the committee's report, which included the compromise "settlement."

When the MFDP representatives heard what had happened, they were furious. Using borrowed admission tickets, the group swarmed onto the convention floor, where some of them occupied the seats designated for Mississippi's regular Democrats, some of whom had already left. The confrontation might easily have erupted into an ugly brawl. But President Lyndon Johnson, worried about the effect of televised mayhem on the voting

During more than five years as president of the United States, Lyndon B. Johnson (1908-1973) earned a reputation as a supporter of civil rights.

public, ordered the security personnel not to evict the demonstrators.

Hamer saw nothing wrong with her behavior in Atlantic City and remained rigidly uncompromising. She was persistent, too, and was one of three MFDP women who carried on a prolonged battle to win seats in the U.S. House of Representatives in the 1964 election. After losing the Democratic primaries in June, the three tried to get on the ballot for the November general election as independents, but they were unsuccessful.

When the new Congress convened in January 1965, they challenged the election results, arguing that Mississippi laws discriminated against blacks. After hearing the women's arguments, the House voted to seat the winners of the contested elections temporarily while a committee investigated the matter. After the committee completed its investigation, the House rejected the women's challenge by a vote of 228 to 143. (Ten House members, including all 5 from Mississippi, simply voted "present," and 51 did not vote at all.)

In 1967, Hamer was one of about a dozen blacks who tried to run for the state senate as independents. The election officials, citing a 1966 change in Mississippi's election laws that made it harder for people to run for public office as independents, refused to place their names on the ballot. The group then filed suit in federal court, claiming that Mississippi's 1966 law violated the Voting Rights Act of 1965, which required federal approval of proposed changes in state election laws in some instances. In March 1969, the U.S. Supreme Court suspended several Mississippi election laws (including the 1966 election law) until the state could prove that these laws didn't discriminate against blacks. The Court, however, allowed the results of elections that were already held under these laws to stand.

In 1971, Hamer again ran for the state senate. Members of the National Women's Political Caucus (an activist group that she had helped to organize earlier that year) helped her try to win, but two-term incumbent Robert Crook defeated her by a margin of about 4,500 votes.

The 1971 campaign was Hamer's last attempt to win an elective office. She never completely abandoned her reform efforts, however. Despite her increasingly poor health, she continued to organize antipoverty projects for Sunflower County residents, monitor school desegregation, and urge prison reform. She also maintained her connection with Democratic national politics.

During the Democratic National Convention of 1972, she was part of a losing effort to nominate Frances Farenthold (a Texas state legislator) for the vice-presidential position on the ticket. In one of her last political acts, Hamer led the singing at an October 1976 rally in Jackson, Mississippi, protesting the imposition of new requirements on those seeking assistance under the Medicaid program.

Fannie Lou Hamer died on March 14, 1977. Many of her old civil rights associates (several of whom had achieved national prominence in public life) gathered in Ruleville for her funeral. The rites ended with a spirited rendition of her favorite freedom song, "This Little Light of Mine."

Feminist Gloria Steinem, one of the nation's most popular women's rights activist, has become a role model for many young women.

8

Gloria Steinem
A Liberated Woman

On September 7, 1968, a group of women marched down Atlantic City's boardwalk in a noisy demonstration. The demonstrators weren't demanding political rights for black Americans, as civil rights activist Fannie Lou Hamer and others had done there four years earlier. Instead, they were protesting against the annual Miss America Pageant. While opponents jeered from behind police barricades, the women tossed women's magazines, girdles, bras, and other items into a "Freedom Trash Can." They later brought out a live sheep and crowned it "Miss America." That evening, as the television cameras focused on the real Miss America, protesters unfurled a large white banner bearing the words "Women's Liberation."

The televised spectacle brought U.S. viewers face to face with the third massive social upheaval of the turbulent 1960s: the women's liberation movement. (The first upheaval was the civil rights movement, and the second was the protest against U.S. participation in the war in Vietnam.)

Although the Atlantic City demonstrators represented only a small minority of those who advocated increased rights for women, many Americans concluded that all "women's libbers" were crazy radicals who were out of touch with mainstream U.S. values. Eventually, though, the woman who came to symbolize the movement best wasn't a wild, unkempt radical as many people had imagined. Instead, she was a poised and successful young journalist named Gloria Steinem.

Steinem's road to success was far from smooth. The second of Leo and Ruth Nuneviller Steinem's two children was born in Toledo, Ohio, on March 25, 1934. The Steinems' first child, Susanne, was almost ten years old when Gloria Marie was born. Today's psychologists would probably describe the family as deeply troubled. Ruth Nuneviller Steinem, who had once worked as a society reporter and editor on a Toledo newspaper, suffered from recurring spells of depression and anxiety that occasionally required her hospitalization. Leo Steinem was a dreamer who operated an entertainment hall in a Michigan summer resort when he wasn't traveling around the country, buying and selling antiques. Gloria's early years alternated between summers at the Michigan resort and trips to California in the family trailer during the winter months. As a result, she attended school only intermittently.

In 1945, the Steinems divorced, and Leo moved to California, where he died in an automobile accident in 1962. When the Steinems' marriage ended, Susanne was attending Smith College in Amherst, Massachusetts. Ruth and Gloria moved to Amherst to be near her, but they later returned to Toledo, where they lived in an upstairs apartment in the house where Ruth had lived as a child.

Both the house and the Toledo neighborhood had deteriorated. So had Ruth's mental condition. There were relatives in Toledo to help, but 12-year-old Gloria, living in a rat-infested house with a mentally ill woman, assumed the full burden of her mother's care. Their main source of income was the rent from the downstairs apartment.

When Gloria was about 16, Susanne persuaded their father to assume responsibility for their mother for a year so Gloria could finish high school in Washington, D.C., where Susanne now lived. Around that time, a local church bought their house in Toledo, and the money from the sale helped to pay Gloria's tuition at Smith College, which she entered in 1952.

Steinem majored in government and politics. An excellent student, she won a fellowship to study in India following her 1956 graduation. She became engaged during her senior year, but broke the engagement after deciding she wasn't ready for marriage.

She did not know she was pregnant until after arriving in London to wait for permission to live in India. She considered returning home to marry her former fiance, but she instead found a sympathetic British doctor who performed an abortion. (At that time, abortions were illegal in many countries, and society generally condemned young women who had children outside of marriage.) For many years, Steinem kept her abortion a secret, and she eventually spoke openly about the operation only in an effort to persuade the public that outlawing abortions was bad public policy.

Steinem's two years in India gave her firsthand experience of the grinding poverty many people suffer in the world. On her return to the United States, she wanted to write about her experience so that Americans could understand the dreadful conditions under which so many of the world's people lived. But she found that few publishers were willing to hire women for positions other than clerical or secretarial jobs.

In 1960, Steinem got her first break in journalism when she landed a job on a small New York magazine called *Help! For Tired Minds.* Steinem's editor enjoyed her company and introduced her to his friends. Before long, she was attending parties with prominent New Yorkers. She also began a series of relationships with men that she called "little marriages," but Steinem did not want to take the final step of legally marrying anyone. When a journalist once asked Steinem what she thought about marriage, she replied that marriage made someone legally half a person, and added, "What man wants to live with half a person?"

In 1968, when the Miss America protest took place, Steinem had not yet emerged on the publishing scene as an advocate of women's rights. Her best-known piece of writing to that point had been a two-part article in 1963 entitled "A Bunny's Tale." In the article, she described her undercover stint working as a "bunny" in *Playboy* publisher Hugh Hefner's semi-private men's organization called the "Playboy Club." Although Steinem wrote the piece in a light, humorous fashion, the article exposed the difficult working conditions of the clubs' scantily clad female employees. Editors and publishers generally ignored its serious purpose, however, and continued to ask Steinem for what they called "puff pieces."

But things began to change. In 1968, Clay Felker, who had worked as an editor for *Esquire* magazine, asked Steinem to help him start and edit a new magazine entitled *New York.* In addition to her editing duties, Steinem wrote a column called the "City Politic," which discussed

Journalist Gloria Steinem wrote one of her most famous articles, "A Bunny's Tale," in 1963 after working undercover as a Playboy bunny.

current political issues and profiled important political figures such as 1968 presidential candidates Richard Nixon and Eugene McCarthy.

In 1969, Steinem wrote an article for *New York* that showed how her ideas on women's issues were evolving. In the article, "After Black Power, Women's Liberation," Steinem argued that the women's liberation movement was an attempt to liberate both men and women from the restrictive roles that society had assigned to them. The article earned her the Penney-Missouri Journalism Award in 1970.

As Steinem's feminist philosophy developed, she and other feminists discussed the possibility of starting a new women's magazine. The traditional women's magazines—managed by men—published articles on fashion, home decorating, cooking, and similar topics that the editors thought would interest women.

Steinem and her friends wanted to see a women's magazine—written and edited by women—that would cover more serious issues that affected them. Steinem got her chance when Clay Felker offered to publish the first issue of *Ms.* as a supplement to *New York's* December 1971 issue. (The magazine's title came from a secretarial handbook that recommended using the term Ms. rather than Miss or Mrs. when a woman's marital status was unknown.)

In January 1972, the first full issue of *Ms.* magazine appeared on newsstands. Originally intended as a "one-shot" publication, the magazine sold out almost immediately. By 1973, *Ms.* had almost 200,000 subscribers. Steinem worked as an editor of *Ms.* until 1987, when the magazine was sold to an Australian publisher, and contributed many articles on various women's issues.

With the appearance of of *Ms.* in January 1972, a more traditional women's magazine, *McCall's*, chose Steinem as its 1972 Woman of the Year. *McCall's*

The January 1973 issue of Ms. *magazine featured a cover*
story on Texas state legislator Frances Farenthold (left), who
tried running for vice-president in 1972, and New York
congresswoman Shirley Chisholm, who campaigned for
president that year.

described Steinem as "the women's movement's most persuasive evangelist . . . preaching a new-found feminism."

By that time, Steinem had helped to organize the National Women's Political Caucus (NWPC), which began in 1971 as a vehicle for getting more women elected to public office. Steinem drafted the NWPC's statement of principles, which included opposition to racism, the repudiation of violence as an acceptable means of settling conflicts, and the establishment of women's reproductive freedom, a term Steinem used for abortion rights.

During the 1972 Democratic National Convention, the NWPC tried to get the party to endorse women's reproductive freedom in its platform. The NWPC didn't succeed, but they did get the Democrats to include a general statement on women's issues in their party platform. Before then, both Republican and Democratic platforms had generally ignored women's issues.

One of Steinem's biggest crusades was her push for the adoption of the Equal Rights Amendment (ERA). Under pressure from Steinem and other feminists, the U.S. House of Representatives passed the ERA in October 1971, and in March 1972 the Senate followed suit. Following a practice that began with the Eighteenth Amendment, Congress allowed a seven-year period for the 50 states to ratify the ERA. (Thirty-eight states had to ratify the ERA to make it part of the Constitution.)

Gloria Steinem, a popular and thought-provoking speaker, addresses the National Women's Political Caucus at the 1972 Democratic Convention.

Steinem campaigned for the ERA in a series of articles, interviews, lectures, and television appearances. For a time, its ratification seemed almost assured. By the spring of 1973, the ERA's supporters needed favorable votes from only a handful of states to achieve their goal.

Opposition to the ERA soon developed, however. In late 1972, Phyllis Schlafly, a conservative Republican activist, formed a national committee to stop passage of the ERA. Schlafly argued that the ERA would destroy the traditional protections that women in the United States already enjoyed, such as legal requirements that husbands support their wives. She also pointed out that

Unlike Gloria Steinem, Phyllis Schlafly argued that the Equal Rights Amendment would take away rights that women already had.

Steinem speaks out in favor of the ERA at a rally in New York City.

by making matters such as marriage, divorce, child custody, and adoption subject to federal authority, the ERA would destroy most of the states' remaining rights.

By the beginning of 1978, favorable votes in only three more states would make the ERA part of the Constitution. The amendment was losing ground, however. In that year, two key states, Virginia and Illinois, failed to ratify it. Moreover, the time period for ratification would expire in 1979.

With time running out, the National Organization for Women (NOW), a feminist group that formed in

1966, organized a massive demonstration in Washington, D.C., to get Congress to extend the ratification period. Steinem played a prominent part in the Women's March, walking at the head of the line and addressing the group afterward. Responding to the women's pressure, Congress extended the ratification deadline to June 30, 1982. But the extension didn't help. When the extended period expired, the ERA still hadn't picked up the 38 votes necessary for ratification.

Although she has had her share of disappointments, Gloria Steinem has retained a positive outlook on life.

Gloria Steinem (left) and editor Pat Carbine celebrate Ms. *magazine's tenth anniversary.*

Steinem, who emerged as a leading women's rights activist during the 1970s, rallies against pornography at an anti-violence demonstration in New York City.

One of her most gratifying experiences was speaking at the Antioch School of Law's 1978 graduation ceremony when her sister, Susanne Steinem Patch, received a degree. Ruth Steinem, whose mental illness had been in remission for some time, was there, too. But Ruth Steinem's general health was failing, and she died in 1981.

One of Gloria Steinem's greatest assets during her career as a journalist and public speaker has been her ability to present controversial issues in terms that average Americans can understand and appreciate. Steinem prefers a friendly conversation to an argument, and she is apt to treat controversy with a joke and a smile. Her goals, however, remain serious: maintaining women's reproductive freedom, encouraging both parents to share in child-rearing, and persuading society to value "women's work" and treat women's lives and problems as seriously as men's. Steinem's books, which include *Outrageous Acts of Everyday Rebellions*, *Revolution from Within*, and *Moving Beyond Words*, have dealt with the issues of sexism and self-esteem.

Like many other women reformers, Steinem believes that race and gender discrimination are intertwined. In her opinion, "These two deepest of all revolutions must be fought together, or both will fail."

The United States has still not achieved the goals of racial and gender equality that reforming women such as Steinem have embraced. Many of the specific changes these reformers want are controversial. No national consensus exists on the issues of abortion, women's role in the workplace, or men's role in child care. Though it is possible that Americans will never achieve a consensus on such controversial issues, reformers are unlikely to give up their attempts to create a society in which no one has second-class status because of race or sex.

Despite tremendous opposition, Gloria Steinem and other activists have tried for years to remain optimistic about the future.

Major Reforms in U.S. History

Important events, laws, and organizations mentioned in this book appear in chronological order:

1775 The American Revolution begins (ends 1783)

1787 Signing of the U.S. Constitution

1807 The U.S. slave trade ends, but slavery continues

1831 Abolitionist William Lloyd Garrison publishes the first issue of the *Liberator*

1833 Formation of the American Anti-Slavery Society

1833 Oberlin College becomes the first college in the United States to admit women

1840 Formation of the American and Foreign Anti-Slavery Society

1848 Suffragists hold the first women's rights convention in Seneca Falls, New York

1850s State and local laws begin placing restrictions on alcohol

1861 The U.S. Civil War begins (ends 1865)

1863 The Emancipation goes into effect on January 1

1865 Passage of the Thirteenth Amendment, which outlaws slavery

1867 Howard University, the first university for blacks, opens in Washington, D.C.

1868 Passage of the Fourteenth Amendment, which states that everyone born or naturalized in the United States is a U.S. citizen

1869 Formation of the National Woman Suffrage Association (NWSA) and the American Woman Suffrage Association (AWSA)

1870 Passage of the Fifteenth Amendment, which says that people cannot be stopped from voting because of their race, color, or previous servitude

1874 Formation of the Woman's Christian Temperance Union

1890 Formation of the National American Woman Suffrage Association (NAWSA) when the NWSA and the AWSA merge

1893 Formation of the Anti-Saloon League

1902 The International Woman Suffrage Alliance is formed

1909 Formation of the National Association for the Advancement of Colored People (NAACP)

1914 World War I begins (ends 1918)

1915 Formation of the Woman's Peace Party

1916 Formation of the National Woman's Party by members of the NAWSA

1919 Formation of the League of Nations

1919 Passage of the Eighteenth Amendment, which outlaws selling, manufacturing, and drinking alcohol

1920 Passage of the Nineteenth Amendment, which gives women the right to vote

1920 Formation of the League of Women Voters

1923 The Equal Rights Amendment is first introduced in Congress

1925 The Committee on the Cause and Cure for War is formed

1929 The stock market crashes, sending the nation into the Great Depression

1933 Passage of the Twenty-first Amendment, which reverses the Eighteenth Amendment and makes alcohol legal again

1933 Frances Perkins becomes U.S. secretary of labor, the first woman appointed to a presidential cabinet

1935 The Social Security Act establishes unemployment insurance and creates government assistance to the elderly

1938 The Fair Labor Standards Act establishes the minimum wage

1946 The United Nations, which replaced the League of Nations, holds its first meeting

1954 The U.S. Supreme Court rules in *Brown v. The Board of Education of Topeka* that "separate-but-equal" schools are unconstitutional

1960 The Student Nonviolent Coordinating Committee (SNCC) forms, and its members begin holding sit-ins to end segregation

1961 The Congress of Racial Equality (CORE), which formed in 1942, organized the first "freedom rides" in the South

1963 200,000 people march on Washington to lobby for civil rights laws

1964 SNCC and other groups organize "Freedom Summer" to end racial segregation

1964 Passage of the Civil Rights Act that outlaws racial discrimination in public accommodations

1965 The Voting Rights Act outlaws literacy tests and other tests designed to keep people from voting

1966 Formation of the National Organization of Women (NOW)

1967 Thurgood Marshall becomes the first African American appointed to the U.S. Supreme Court (Clarence Thomas becomes the second in 1992)

1969 U.S. troop levels reach a high of nearly 550,000 during the Vietnam War

1972 The first issue of *Ms.* magazine appears on newsstands

1973 The Supreme Court rules in *Roe v. Wade* that abortion is legal during the first three months of pregnancy

1981 Sandra Day O'Connor becomes the first woman on the U.S. Supreme Court (Ruth Bader Ginsburg becomes the second in 1993)

1982 The Equal Rights Amendment is defeated in Congress, but political activists continue making reforms in the United States

Bibliography

Adams, Mildred. "Carrie Chapman Catt." *The Nation,* March 22, 1947.

Baker, Paula. "The Domestication of Politics: Women and American Political Society, 1780-1920." *American Historical Review,* June 1984.

Belfrage, Sally. *Freedom Summer.* New York: Viking Press, 1965.

Bordin, Ruth. *Frances Willard: A Biography.* Chapel Hill: University of North Carolina Press, 1986.

Cagin, Seth and Philip Dray. *We Are Not Afraid: The Story of Goodman, Schwerner, and Chaney, and the Civil Rights Campaign for Mississippi.* New York: Macmillan, 1988.

Chafe, William H. *The Paradox of American Change: Women in the 20th Century.* New York: Oxford University Press, 1991.

Cohen, Marcia. *The Sisterhood: The True Story of the Women Who Changed the World.* New York: Simon and Schuster, 1988.

Dillon, Mary Earhart. "Willard, Frances Elizabeth Caroline." *Notable American Women,* vol. III, ed. Edward T. James. Cambridge: Harvard University Press, 1971.

Feeley, Malcolm M., and Samuel Krislov, eds. *Constitutional Law.* Boston: Little, Brown & Co., 1985.

Flexnor, Eleanor. "Catt, Carrie Clinton Lane Chapman." *Notable American Women*, vol I., ed. Edward T. James. Cambridge: Harvard University Press, 1971.

Fowler, Robert Booth. *Carrie Catt: Feminist Politician.* Boston: Northeastern University Press, 1986.

Giddings, Paula. "Ida Wells-Barnett." *Portraits of American Women*, ed. G. J. Barker-Benfield and Catherine Clinton. New York: St. Martin's Press, 1991.

"Gloria Steinem." *Newsweek*, August 16, 1971.

Grant, Jacquelyn. "Fannie Lou Hamer." *Notable Black American Women*. Detroit: Gale Research Inc., 1992.

Henry, Sondra and Emily Taitz. *One Woman's Power: A Biography of Gloria Steinem*. Minneapolis: Dillon Press, 1987.

Hoff, Mark. *Gloria Steinem: The Women's Movement.* Brookfield, CT: The Millbrook Press, 1991.

Holt, Thomas C. "The Lonely Warrior: Ida B. Wells-Barnett and the Struggle for Black Leadership." *Black Leaders of the Twentieth Century*, ed. John Hope Franklin and August Meier. Urbana: University of Illinois Press, 1982.

Kerber, Linda K. "Judge Ginsburg's Gift." *Washington Post*, August 1, 1993.

McAdam, Doug. *Freedom Summer.* New York: Oxford University Press, 1988.

Mills, Kay. *This Little Light of Mine: The Life of Fannie Lou Hamer.* New York: Dutton, 1993.

Murray, Pauli. *Song in a Weary Throat: An American Pilgrimage*. New York: Harper & Row, 1987.

Norton, Mary Beth. "The Evolution of White Women's Experience in Early America." *American Historical Review*, June 1984.

Peck, Mary Gray. *Carrie Chapman Catt: A Biography*. New York: H. W. Wilson Co., 1944.

Roosevelt, Anna Eleanor and Lorena E. Hickok. "A New Deal for Women in Politics." *Ladies of Courage*. New York: G. P. Putnam's Sons, 1954.

Rosenberg, Rosalind. *Divided Lives: American Women in the Twentieth Century*. New York: Hill & Wang, 1992.

Steinem, Gloria. *Outrageous Acts of Everyday Rebellions*. New York: Signet, 1986.

Sterling, Dorothy. *Ahead of Her Time: Abby Kelley and the Politics of Antislavery*. New York: W. W. Norton, 1991.

_____. "Ida B. Wells." *Black Foremothers: Three Lives*, 2nd ed. New York: The Feminist Press, 1988.

Taylor, Paul C. "Dewson, Mary Williams." *Notable American Women: The Modern Period: A Biographical Dictionary*. Cambridge: Harvard University Press, 1980.

Thompson, Mildred. *Ida B. Wells-Barnett: An Exploratory Study of an American Black Woman*. Brooklyn: Carlson Publishing, Inc., 1990.

Truman, Margaret. *Women of Courage*. New York: William Morrow & Co., Inc., 1976.

Van Voris, Jacqueline. *Carrie Chapman Catt: A Public Life*. New York: The Feminist Press, 1987.

Vick, Marsha C. "Pauli Murray." *Notable Black American Women*. Detroit: Gale Research, Inc. 1992.

Ware, Susan. *Beyond Suffrage: Women in the New Deal*. Cambridge: Harvard University Press, 1981.

_____. *Partner and I: Molly Dewson, Feminism and the New Deal*. New Haven: Yale University Press, 1987.

Whitney, Sharon and Tom Raynor. *Women in Politics*. New York: Franklin Watts, 1986.

Woodward, C. Vann. *The Strange Career of Jim Crow*, 3rd rev. ed. New York: Oxford University Press, 1974.

Wynn, Linda T. "Ida B. Wells-Barnett." *Notable Black American Women*. Detroit: Gale Research, Inc., 1992.

Young, Louise M. *In the Public Interest: The League of Women Voters, 1920-1970*. New York: Greenwood Press, 1989.

Zangrando, Robert L. *The NAACP Crusade Against Lynching, 1909-1950*. Philadelphia: Temple University Press, 1980.

Index

"Abby Kelleyism," 20
abolitionists, 8, 13, 15, 16,
17, 21, 23, 25, 57; division
among, 19, 20
abortion, 132, 137, 143
Adams, Charles Francis, 81
alcohol abuse, 28, 36
Allen, Florence, 90
Alpha Suffrage Club, 57
American and Foreign Anti-
Slavery Society, 19-20
American Anti-Slavery
Society, 15, 17, 19, 23, 27
American Civil Liberties
Union, 109, 110
American Woman Suffrage
Association, 73
Anthony, Susan B., 25, 62,
63, 64
Antioch School of Law, 143
Anti-Saloon League, 42

Barnett, Alfreda, 54, 59
Barnett, Ferdinand L., 53,
54
"Boston marriage," 84
Boston Tea Party, 81
Brandeis University, 110
*Brown v. The Board of
Education of Topeka*, 105

Carbine, Pat, 141
Catt, Carrie Chapman, 76,
85; death of, 77; early

years of, 62-63; education
of, 63; as head of National
American Woman
Suffrage Association, 62,
64, 65, 66, 67-68, 70, 71,
73; and League of
Women Voters, 73;
marriages of, 63-64; as
pacifist, 68, 69, 70, 77;
tactics of, in suffragist
movement, 60, 65, 67, 68,
70-71, 73- 74
Catt, George, 64
Chaney, James, 121
Chapman, Leo, 63-64
Chicago Conservator, 53
Chisholm, Shirley, 136
Civil Rights Act (1875), 47
Civil Rights Cases, 47, 48,
105
civil rights movement, 97,
104, 105, 118, 120, 127,
130; early years of, 101,
102, 103, 115; leaders of,
97, 102, 112, 116, 119,
123; organizations active
in, 55, 101-102, 104-105,
116, 118, 120
Civil War, 23, 36, 45, 47, 49,
99
Cleveland, Grover, 57
Committee on Economic
Security, Advisory
Council, 93

Committee on the Cause and Cure of War, 77

Congress, U.S., 17, 42, 47, 68, 71, 73, 108, 125, 137, 141

Congress of Racial Equality (CORE), 116, 121

Constitution, U.S., 19, 27, 61, 71, 108, 137, 140

Consumers' Advisory Board, 90

Crook, Robert, 126

Democratic National Campaign Committee, Women's Division, 88

Democratic National Committee, Women's Division of, 90, 92, 93

Democratic National Convention, 93; in 1956, 97; in 1964, 122-125; in 1972, 126, 137, 138

Democratic party, 57, 65, 67, 87, 90, 93, 97-98, 122-125, 126, 137

Dewson, Edward, 81, 83

Dewson, Elizabeth, 81, 83

Dewson, Mary Williams (Molly), 78; as assistant to Felix Frankfurter, 86; death of, 95; early years of, 81, 83; education of, 83; friendship of, with Eleanor Roosevelt, 79, 80, 81, 86-87, 88, 89, 92, 93, 95; jobs of, 83, 84, 85, 86, 87, 90; relationship of, with Mary (Polly) Porter, 83-85, 87, 90, 94, 95; role of, in national Democratic politics, 79, 81, 87, 88, 89, 90, 92, 93-94; and suffrage movement, 85

Dewson, Molly, *See* Dewson, Mary Williams

Du Bois, W.E.B., 57, 58

Eastland, James, 117

Eighteenth Amendment, 42, 137

Emancipation Proclamation, 24, 45

Episcopal church, 99, 111

Equal Rights Amendment (ERA), 108, 137, 139-141

Esquire, 133

Evanston Ladies College, 35

Fair Labor Standards Act, 86

Farenthold, Frances, 126, 136

Farley, James, 88, 92, 93

Felker, Clay, 133, 135

Fifteenth Amendment, 25, 27

Fitzgerald, Cornelia Smith, 99

Fitzgerald, Pauline, 98, 99

Fitzgerald, Robert, 99

Fitzgerald, Sallie, 99

Foster, Abby Kelley, 57; and antislavery movement, 12,

13, 15, 17-19, 20, 23, 25; death of, 27; early years of, 14-15; education of, 14-15; marriage of, 21; as public speaker, 17-18, 19, 20; as Quaker, 13, 14, 15, 20; support of, for Fifteenth Amendment, 25, 27; and women's rights, 23, 25, 27

Foster, Paulina Wright, 22

Foster, Stephen Symonds, 20-23, 27

Fourteenth Amendment, 47, 105, 108, 109

Fowler, Charles, 32, 35

Frankfurter, Felix, 86, 87

"freedom rides," 116

"Freedom Summer," 120-121

Free Speech and Headlight, 48, 51, 52

Gaines v. Canada, 101

Garrett Theological Seminary, 32

Garrison, William Lloyd, 15, 16, 19, 20, 23

gender discrimination, 9, 107, 108, 109, 143, 144

Ghana, 107-108

Ginsburg, Ruth Bader, 110

Goldwater, Barry, 123

Goodman, Andrew, 120-121

Gordon, Anna, 40, 41

Hamer, Fannie Lou, 129; attack on, in prison, 119-120; and civil rights movement, 112, 113, 118, 119, 126; death of, 127; early years of, 114; and Freedom Summer, 120-121; marriage of, 114; and Mississippi Freedom Democratic Party, 122-125; as political candidate, 125-126; as sharecropper, 114-115, 118; work of, for voter registration, 117-118, 122

Hamer, Perry, 114-115

Harvard Law School, 107

Hayes, Rutherford, 49

Hefner, Hugh, 133

Help! For Tired Minds, 133

Home Protection Ballot, 37

Howard University Law School, 104, 105, 107

Hunter College, 99, 101

International Woman Suffrage Alliance, 64

"Iola," 48, *See also*, Wells-Barnette, Ida

Jackson, Kate, 32

Johnson, Lyndon, 124

Kelley, Albert, 14, 15

Kelley, Lucy, 15, 19

Kelley, Olive, 19

Kennedy, John, 108, 109

King, Martin Luther, Jr., 116

Lane, Lucius, 62
Lane, Maria, 62, 64
League of Nations, 75
League of Women Voters, 73, 75
Liberator, 15
Liberia, 15
Lincoln, Abraham, 23, 24, 45
literacy test, 117-118
Lynch, Charles, 49
lynching, 49, 50-51, 53, 114
Lynn Female Anti-Slavery Society, 17

McCall's, 135
McCarthy, Eugene, 134
McKinley, William, 57
Marshall, Thurgood, 102, 105
Massachusetts State Industrial School for Girls, 82-83
Massachusetts Woman Suffrage Association, 85
Methodist church, 31
minimum wage, 86
Miss America Pageant, 129-130, 133
Mississippi, 114; and Democratic politics, 122-123, 124; segregation in, 116-117, 119, 120-121, 125-126

Mississippi Freedom Democratic party (MFDP), 122-125
Montgomery, Alabama, bus boycott in, 116
Morgan v. Virginia, 103
Moving Beyond Words, 143
Ms., 135, 136, 141
Murray, Agnes Fitzgerald, 98
Murray, Anna Pauline (Pauli), 96; death of, 111; early years of, 98, 99, 100, 101; education of, 99, 101-102, 104, 105, 107, 108; efforts of, to end racial discrimination, 101-103, 104, 105; as Episcopal priest, 111; friendship of, with Eleanor Roosevelt, 105-107; as lawyer, 107; racial heritage of, 98, 99; as teacher, 108, 110; and women's rights, 107, 108-109, 110
Murray, Pauli, *See* Murray, Anna Pauline
Murray, William, 98-99

Nation, The, 77
National American Woman Suffrage Association (NAWSA), 62, 64, 65, 66, 67, 85; campaign of, for women's suffrage, 68, 70-71

National Association for the Advancement of Colored People (NAACP), 55, 58, 101-102, 104-105
National Consumers' League, 86
National Organization for Women (NOW), 140-141
National Woman Suffrage Association, 73
National Woman's Party, 71, 108
National Women's Political Caucus, 126, 137, 138
New York, 133-134, 135
New York Age, 51, 52, 53
Nineteenth Amendment, 7, 9, 61, 73, 74
Nixon, Richard, 134
North Western Female College, 31, 35
Northwestern University, 31, 35

Oberlin College, 30
Outrageous Acts of Everyday Rebellions, 143
Owen, Ruth Bryan, 90

Paul, Alice, 65, 71, 72
Pauli Murray Scholarship, 111
Peck, Mary Gray, 61
Penney-Missouri Journalism Award, 135
People's party, 38
Perkins, Frances, 90, 91

Playboy Club, 133, 134
Plessy v. Ferguson, 105
political office, women in, 9, 27, 57, 89-90, 94, 137
Populist party, 38
Porter, Mary (Polly), 83-85, 87, 90, 94, 95
President's Commission on the Status on Women (PCSW), 108
Prohibition, 42, 43
Prohibition party, 36, 38, 42

Quakers, 14, 20

racial discrimination, 9, 47, 48, 100, 107, 112, 143, 144
rape, 40; of white women, 51, 53
Red Cross, 85
Reed v. Reed, 109-110
reproductive freedom, 10-11, 137, 143
Republican party, 23, 57, 67, 123, 137, 139
Revolution from Within, 143
Roosevelt, Betsy, 82
Roosevelt, Eleanor, 79, 80, 81, 82, 86, 88, 89, 92, 93, 95, 106, 108; role in Democratic party, 87, 97-98, 105, 106, 107
Roosevelt, Franklin, 82, 87, 88, 89, 93-94

Schlafly, Phyllis, 139

Schwerner, Michael, 121
segregation, 47, 97-98, 114, 115, 125-126; efforts to end, 47, 48, 101, 102, 103, 104, 105, 116, 119, 120-121
Seneca Falls, New York, meeting in, 23, 62
Seward, William, 24
sexual harassment, 11
sharecroppers, 114-115
Shaw, Anna Howard, 65, 66
"sit-ins," 116
slavery, 13, 15, 17, 18, 23, 24, 25, 45, 47; movement to abolish, 8, 12, 13, 15, 17, 19-20
Smith, Alfred, 79, 81
Smith, Sidney, 99
Smith College, 131, 132
Social Security Act, 93
Social Security Board, 93
Society of Friends, 14, 20
Southern Christian Leadership Conference (SCLC), 116
Stanton, Elizabeth Cady, 25, 26, 62
Steinem, Leo, 130, 131
Steinem, Gloria: campaign of, for passage of ERA, 137, 139-141; early years of, 130-132; education of, 131-132; experience of, in India, 132; as journalist and writer, 132-135, 143; and *Ms.* magazine, 135, 141; and National Political Women's Caucus, 137, 138; as Playboy bunny, 133, 134; and women's rights, 6, 128, 134-135, 142, 143, 144
Steinem, Ruth Nuneviller, 130-131, 143
Steinem, Susanne, 130, 131, 143
Student Nonviolent Coordinating Committee (SNCC), 116, 118; voter registration campaign of, 118, 120-121
suffrage, women's, 25, 37, 38, 57, 64-65; efforts to achieve, 60, 61-62, 67-68, 70-71, 73, 74, 85
Supreme Court, U.S., 86, 90, 93, 109-110; decisions of, in civil rights cases, 47, 48, 97, 101, 102, 103, 104-105, 116, 126

temperance movement, 28, 35, 36-38, 40, 42
Thirteenth Amendment, 25
Townsend, James, 114
Townsend, Lou Ella, 114
Twenty-first Amendment, 42, 43

United Nations, 77
University of California, 107
University of North

Carolina, 101-102, 111
U.S. v. Darby, 86

Vietnam War, 130
voting rights, 7, 9; for
  blacks, 25, 26, 27, 47, 57,
  113, 114, 116-118, 120-
  121, 125; for women, 7, 9,
  25, 26, 27, 37, 38, 57, 61-
  62, 64-65, 67-68, 70-71,
  73, 78, 85
Voting Rights Act of 1965,
  125-126

Washington, Booker T., 55,
  56
Wellesley College, 83
Wells, James, 45-46
Wells, Lizzie, 45, 46
Wells-Barnett, Ida, 44, 54,
  105, 114; crusade of,
  against lynching, 49, 50-
  51, 53, 55, 57, 59; death
  of, 57; early years of, 45,
  46; education of, 46; and
  formation of NAACP, 55;
  marriage of, 53; as a
  newspaper reporter and
  editor, 48, 50-53, 55; as
  teacher, 46, 47, 48-49; and
  women's suffrage, 57
Willard, Frances (Frank)
  Elizabeth, 28, 34, 39;
  death of, 40, 41, early
  years of, 30-31; education
  of, 30-31; as leader of
  Woman's Christian

Temperance Union, 35,
  37, 38, 40, 42; and
  Prohibition party, 38; as
  teacher, 29, 32, 33, 35, 37;
  and women's suffrage, 37,
  38
Willard, Josiah, 30, 31, 32
Willard, Mary (Frances
  Willard's sister), 30, 31,
  34, 35
Willard, Mary Hill (Frances
  Willard's mother), 30, 34,
  35
Willard, Oliver, 30, 35
Wilson, Woodrow, 57, 68,
  69, 71
Woman's Christian Tem-
  perance Union (WCTU),
  35, 36-37, 38, 40
Woman's Peace Party, 70
Women's Action Committee
  for Victory and Lasting
  Peace, 77
Women's City Club of New
  York, 86, 87
Women's Educational and
  Industrial Union, 83
women's rights, 9, 10-11, 23,
  25, 26, 27, 62, 128, 133,
  134-135, 137, 142, 143
women's suffrage, *See*
  suffrage, women's
World War I, 68, 70-71, 75,
  85
World War II, 77, 115

Yale Law School, 108

Photo Credits

Photographs courtesy of Bettye Lane Studio: pp. 6, 138, 139, 140, 141, 142, 144; Library of Congress, pp. 12, 18, 24, 26, 34, 41, 58, 66, 69, 72, 74, 76, 87, 91, 94, 103, 109, 117, 123; Minnesota Historical Society, pp. 16, 26, 28, 43, 49, 56, 63; The Library Company of Philadelphia, pp. 21, 22; National Woman's Christian Temperance Union, Evanston, Illinois, pp. 33, 39; Schomburg Center for Research in Black Culture, pp. 44, 52, 54, 96; League of Women Voters of the United States, pp. 60, 67, 70, 75; Franklin D. Roosevelt Library, pp. 78, 80, 82, 89, 92, 106; The Schlesinger Library, Radcliffe College, p. 100; Supreme Court Historical Society, pp. 102, 110; The Bettmann Archive, pp. 112, 121 (all); Mississippi Department of Archives and History, p. 115 (both); Amistad Research Center, p. 119; Lyndon Baines Johnson Library, p. 124; Gloria Steinem, p. 128; Playboy Enterprises (Copyright 1973), p. 134.

ABOUT THE AUTHOR

ISOBEL V. MORIN, a native of Patchogue, New York, got a "worm's eye" view of national politics while working as a civil servant for the federal government. After retiring in 1985, she enrolled in graduate school at the University of Maryland in Baltimore County, where she received a master's degree in historical studies. She is the author of *Women of the U.S. Congress* and the forthcoming book, *Women Chosen for Public Office*.